POEMS

BY

ROSE TERRY.

BOSTON:
TICKNOR AND FIELDS.
M DCCC LXI.

RIVERSIDE, CAMBRIDGE:
STEREOTYPED AND PRINTED BY H. O. HOUGHTON.

POEMS

BY

ROSE TERRY

BOSTON:
TICKNOR AND FIELDS.
M DCCC LXI.

RIVERSIDE, CAMBRIDGE:
STEREOTYPED AND PRINTED BY H. O. HOUGHTON.

CONTENTS.

POEMS.

BALLADS.

TRANSLATIONS.

POEMS.

TRAILING ARBUTUS.

Darlings of the forest!
  Blossoming alone
When Earth's grief is sorest
  For her jewels gone —
Ere the last snow-drift melts, your tender buds have blown.

Tinged with color faintly,
  Like the morning sky,
Or more pale and saintly,
  Wrapped in leaves ye lie,
Even as children sleep in faith's simplicity.

There the wild wood-robin
  Hymns your solitude,
And the rain comes sobbing
  Through the budding wood,
While the low south wind sighs, but dare not be more rude.

Were your pure lips fashioned
  Out of air and dew:
Starlight unimpassioned,
  Dawn's most tender hue —
And scented by the woods that gathered sweets for you?

Fairest and most lonely,
  From the world apart,
Made for beauty only,
  Veiled from Nature's heart,
With such unconscious grace as makes the dream of Art!

Were not mortal sorrow
  An immortal shade,
Then would I to-morrow
  Such a flower be made,
And live in the dear woods where my lost childhood played.

ONCE BEFORE.

Sole she sat beside her window,
  Hearing only rain-drops pour,
  Looking only at the shore,
When, outside the little casement,
Weeping in a feigned abasement,
  Love stood knocking —
Knocking at her bolted door.

Slow she swung the little casement
  Where the Autumn roses glowed,
  Sweet and sad her deep eyes showed ;
And her voice, in gentlest measure,
Said aloud — " Nor Love, nor Pleasure
  Can come in here any more —
Never, any more ! "

" But I am not Love nor Pleasure —
  I am but an orphan baby;
  Lost, my mother is, or maybe
Dead she lies, while I am weeping,"

Sobbed the child, his soft lie creeping
  Softly through the bolted door —
Through the maiden's door.

Low she said, in accents lonely:
  "Once I let him in before,
  Once I opened wide my door.
Ever since my life is dreary,
All my prayers are vague and weary;
  Once I let him in before,
Now I'll double-lock the door!"

In the rain he stands imploring;
  Tears and kisses storm the door,
  Where she let him in before.
Will she never know repenting?
Will she ever, late relenting,
  Let him in, as once before?
Will she double-lock the door?

BEYOND.

The stranger wandering in the Switzer's land,
  Before its awful mountain tops afraid, —
Who yet, with patient toil, hath gained his stand,
  On the bare summit where all life is stayed,

Sees far, far down, beneath his blood-dimmed eyes,
  Another country, golden to the shore,
Where a new passion and new hopes arise,
  Where Southern blooms unfold forevermore.

And I, lone sitting by the twilight blaze,
  Think of another wanderer in the snows,
And on more perilous mountain-tops I gaze,
  Than ever frowned above the vine and rose.

Yet courage, soul! nor hold thy strength in vain,
  In hope o'ercome the steeps God set for thee;
For past the Alpine summits of great pain,
  Lieth thine Italy.

"IT IS MORE BLESSED."

Give! as the morning that flows out of heaven;
Give! as the waves when their channel is riven;
Give! as the free air and sunshine are given;
  Lavishly, utterly, carelessly give.
Not the waste drops of thy cup overflowing,
Not the faint sparks of thy hearth ever glowing,
Not a pale bud from the June rose's blowing;
  Give as He gave thee, who gave thee to live.

Pour out thy love like the rush of a river
Wasting its waters, forever and ever,
Through the burnt sands that reward not the giver;
  Silent or songful, thou nearest the sea.
Scatter thy life as the Summer shower's pouring!
What if no bird through the pearl-rain is soaring?
What if no blossom looks upward adoring?
  Look to the life that was lavished for thee!

Give, though thy heart may be wasted and weary,
Laid on an altar all ashen and dreary;

Though from its pulses a faint miserere
  Beats to thy soul the sad presage of fate,
Bind it with cords of unshrinking devotion;
Smile at the song of its restless emotion;
'Tis the stern hymn of eternity's ocean;
  Hear! and in silence thy future await.

So the wild wind strews its perfumed caresses,
Evil and thankless the desert it blesses,
Bitter the wave that its soft pinion presses,
  Never it ceaseth to whisper and sing.
What if the hard heart give thorns for thy roses?
What if on rocks thy tired bosom reposes?
Sweetest is music with minor-keyed closes,
  Fairest the vines that on ruin will cling.

Almost the day of thy giving is over;
Ere from the grass dies the bee-haunted clover,
Thou wilt have vanished from friend and from lover.
  What shall thy longing avail in the grave?
Give as the heart gives whose fetters are breaking,
Life, love, and hope, all thy dreams and thy waking.
Soon, heaven's river thy soul-fever slaking,
  Thou shalt know God and the gift that he gave.

2

A STORY.

In a gleam of sunshine a gentian stood,
  Dreaming her life away,
While the leaves danced merrily through the wood,
  And rode on the wind for play.

She stood in the light and looked at the sky,
  Till her leaves were as fair a blue;
But she shut her heart from the butterfly
  And the coaxing drops of dew.

Dreaming and sunning that autumn noon,
  She stayed the idlest bee
That ever lingered to hear the tune
  Of the wind in a rustling tree.

He had a golden cuirass on,
  And a surcoat black as night,
And he wandered ever from shade to sun,
  Seeking his own delight.

Now were the blossoms of Summer fled,
  And the bumble-bee felt the frost;
He knew that the asters all lay dead,
  And the honey-vine cups were lost.

So he poised and fluttered above the flower,
  And tried his tenderest arts,
With whispers and kisses, a weary hour,
  Till he opened its heart of hearts.

Not for love of the gentian blue,
  But for his own wild will;
All he wanted was honey-dew,
  And there he drank his fill.

No more dreaming in sun or shade!
  It never could close again!
The gentian withered, alone, dismayed;
  The bee flew over the plain.

BLUE-BEARD'S CLOSET.

FASTEN the chamber!
Hide the red key;
Cover the portal,
That eyes may not see.
Get thee to market,
To wedding and prayer;
Labor or revel,
The chamber is there!

In comes a stranger—
"Thy pictures how fine,
Titian or Guido,
Whose is the sign?"
Looks he behind them?
Ah! have a care!
"Here is a finer."
The chamber is there!

Fair spreads the banquet,
Rich the array;

See the bright torches
Mimicking day;
When harp and viol
Thrill the soft air,
Comes a light whisper:
The chamber is there!

Marble and painting,
Jasper and gold,
Purple from Tyrus,
Fold upon fold,
Blossoms and jewels,
Thy palace prepare:
Pale grows the monarch;
The chamber is there!

Once it was open
As shore to the sea;
White were the turrets,
Goodly to see;
All through the casements
Flowed the sweet air;
Now it is darkness;
The chamber is there!

Silence and horror
Brood on the walls;

Through every crevice
A little voice calls:
"Quicken, mad footsteps,
On pavement and stair;
Look not behind thee,
The chamber is there!"

Out of the gateway,
Through the wide world,
Into the tempest
Beaten and hurled,
Vain is thy wandering,
Sure thy despair,
Flying or staying,
The chamber is there!

THE LESSON.

FLUTTER thy new wings lightly,
Poor, fearful little bird!
Nor grasp thy bough so tightly;
Hast thou not heard
That flood of loving song wherewith the leaves are stirred?

Still poised: afraid of flying!
What softer mother-call,
Through the warm sunshine crying,
Could woo thee not to fall?
Doth not its sweetness say, — "Dear child, fear not at all?"

Now the cool wind shall aid thee;
Spread thy new wings and fly!
The master-hand that made thee,
Gave heart and wings to try.
The worst fate that befalls can only be to die.

Ah! from the light branch springing,
  My little darling flies,
And that low, tender singing
  In tenderer silence dies,
While with adventurous plume her nestling tempts the skies.

His new-discovered pinions
  Shall bear thy bird away,
Into those far dominions,
  Beyond the dawning day,
And thou, poor mother-heart, in solitude shalt stay.

Yet some most weary proving
  Taught him to spread the wing,
And some most lonely loving
  Taught thee such notes to sing.
God keep both song and strength to decorate His Spring!

FRATERNITÉ.

Crœsus, gilt martyr of a bank,
  Barred round with ingots yellow,
The poet whom you do not thank,
  Is not a "wretched fellow"!
The garret of his dreaming sleep
  Is tapestried with splendor,
Whose glitter makes no angels weep;
  His heart is true and tender.

Poet, the Dives you despise
  Has pleasure in his money!
Dear butterfly, some beauty lies
  To bees in making honey!
The gold and jewels of your flowers
  He copies in his treasure;
Must all your brother's happy hours
  Be meted with your measure?

Fair woman, whose averted eyes
  Cast scorn on shame's poor daughter,

The soul whose kindred yours denies
  Was limpid once as water!
Who kept thee from the precipice,
  Where sin with love-lips kissed her?
Through Him who granted Mary's peace,
  Pray for thy wretched sister!

And thou, on earth most desolate,
  Blame not the passer by thee,
Whose veiled eyes droop not out of hate,
  Whose thoughts no love deny thee!
If custom-kept, she walks apart,
  Her pity grows the stronger;
And louder echo through her heart
  His words, — "Go, sin no longer."

If there are mountains in the world,
  Are there not also valleys!
Where Love's blue standard swings unfurled,
  There every true heart rallies.
Ranked in one hope, the difference dies
  That keeps us from each other,
And underneath millennial skies,
  Each man becomes a brother.

THE TWO VILLAGES.

Over the river, on the hill,
Lieth a village white and still;
All around it the forest-trees
Shiver and whisper in the breeze;
Over it sailing shadows go
Of soaring hawk and screaming crow,
And mountain grasses, low and sweet,
Grow in the middle of every street.

Over the river, under the hill,
Another village lieth still;
There I see in the cloudy night
Twinkling stars of household light,
Fires that gleam from the smithy's door,
Mists that curl on the river-shore;
And in the roads no grasses grow,
For the wheels that hasten to and fro.

In that village on the hill
Never is sound of smithy or mill;

The houses are thatched with grass and flowers;
Never a clock to toll the hours;
The marble doors are always shut,
You cannot enter in hall or hut;
All the villagers lie asleep;
Never a grain to sow or reap;
Never in dreams to moan or sigh;
Silent and idle and low they lie.

In that village under the hill,
When the night is starry and still,
Many a weary soul in prayer
Looks to the other village there,
And weeping and sighing, longs to go
Up to that home from this below;
Longs to sleep in the forest wild,
Whither have vanished wife and child,
And heareth, praying, this answer fall:
"Patience! that village shall hold ye all!"

WOOD WORSHIP.

HERE, in the silent forest solitudes,
  Deep in the quiet of these lonely shades,
The angelic peace of heaven forever broods,
  And His own presence fills the solemn glades.

Cease, my weak soul, the courts of men to tread,
  Leave the tumultuous heavings of thy kind,
And, by the soul of grateful nature led,
  Seek the still woods and there thy Sabbath find.

Shall worship only live in pillared domes, —
  The organ's pealing notes sole anthems raise, —
While every wind that through the forest roams,
  Draws from its whispering boughs a chant of
      praise?

Here the thick leaves that scent the tremulous air
  Let the bright sunshine pass with softened light,
And lips unwonted breathe instinctive prayer,
  In these cool arches filled with verdurous night.

There needs no bending knee, no costly shrine,
  No fluctuant crowd to hail divinity;
Here the heart kneels, and owns the love divine,
  That made for man the earth so fair and free.

Dear is the choral hymn, the murmuring sound
  Of mutual prayer, and words of holy power;
But give to me the forest's awe profound,
  Æolian hymns, and sermons from a flower!

A NEW VOICE.

THE south-wind blows a wakeful blast,
The hot noon sunshine beams at last,
And something says, — "the past is past."

Come, crocus, from the trodden clay!
Forgotten there for many a day,
Put on thy shining, gold array.

There is no life for death and pain;
There is a new life for the brain
That hears the whispers of the rain.

Dream, crocus, in thy bed of mould;
Feel dimly for thy crown of gold!
Thy fairy-tale shall yet be told.

What if thy lips are cold with fear,
Thy white lids blanched with many a tear?
Awake! an echo wandereth here.

Awake, awake! I hear those calls,
Soft as the desert dew that falls
To stir the acacia's yellow balls.

Love, there is love! For thee too, Spring
Shall a new promise-anthem bring;
Thou art not a forgotten thing.

The shadow of thy bridal veil,
The anguish of the nightingale,
Heaven's passion-fever, makes thee pale;

Though not about thy blue-veined brows
They weave Sicilian orange-boughs;
For thine are all immortal vows.

The Spirit, sun-winged and divine,
That fills the earth-veins full of wine,
And shoots to heaven the bacchant vine, —

The Spirit of all growth and power,
Whose breath informs the sleeping flower,
And speeds the Spring's triumphant hour, —

Creative, jubilant, serene,
Wearing to man a various mien,
Yet true as midnight's crescent queen, —

Unknown of men, yet known to thee,—
Beyond a dim and dawn-lit sea,
That living Spirit stays for thee.

Arise, arise! thy wings begin
To stir their slumberous plumes within:
Hark!—hear'st the bride-song stealing in?

A CHILD'S WISH.

"Be my fairy, mother,
  Give me a wish a day;
Something, as well in sunshine
  As when the rain-drops play."

"And if I were a fairy,
  With but one wish to spare,
What should I give thee, darling,
  To quiet thine earnest prayer?"

"I'd like a little brook, mother,
  All for my very own,
To laugh all day among the trees,
  And shine on the mossy stone;

"To run right under the window,
  And sing me fast asleep,
With soft steps and a tender sound,
  Over the grass to creep.

"Make it run down the hill, mother,
With a leap like a tinkling bell,
So fast I never can catch the leaf
That into its fountain fell.

"Make it as wild as a frightened bird,
As crazy as a bee,
And a noise like the baby's funny laugh;
That's the brook for me!"

FALL.

I HEARD a tree to its sole self complain,
Amid whose robes of rust and scarlet stain
The solemn sunshine poured its golden rain.

Strange as the mournful sounds that steal through
sleep,
As if a mist should strive in dews to weep,
The low, sad cadence past my sense did creep.

"Ah! little, tender, dancing leaves, that first
Out of my sere and wintry branches burst,
With mildest showers and April sunshine nurst;

"More verdant garlands, fresh with life and June,
Wherein the light winds played a fairy tune,
And set them glittering to the quiet moon;

"Then, in their prime, the thick, green summer
leaves,
Lost in whose rustling depth the cricket grieves,
Or the quaint spider radiant tracery weaves;

"Swift ye forsake, slow fluttering to the ground,
These desolate boughs no more with glory crowned,
Where every rain may breathe its sighing sound.

"One, and another, and another yet;
No time for grief to ripen to regret!
Full on my brow stands the sharp coronet.

"Did the cold terror, curdling at my heart,
Strike sudden death, and force your clasp apart,
I too were all too chill to feel ye part.

"But warm and fierce the vital torrent flows,
As keener thorns surround the brightest rose,
Death's bitterest draught life's ardor only knows."

BELL-SONGS. No. 1.

"Funera plango."

Toll, toll, toll! soar, thou passing bell,
Over meadows green and quiet,
Over towns where life runs riot;
Do thine errand well!
Sing thy message, sad and calm,
Cold and holy as a psalm,
Hush us with thy knell!

Toll, toll, toll! over wind and wave:
Through the sunshine's sudden fading,
Through the pine-tree's voice upbraiding,
Where the wild seas rave.
Snow-drifts for the Summer wait;
Slumber for the desolate;
Silence in the grave.

Toll, toll, toll! through the quivering sky;
Chime thy song of wintry weather;
Cruel, through this rapturous ether,
Call the bride to die.

Chill, with thy relentless tongue,
Eyes that smiled and lips that sung;
Bid delight good-bye.

Toll, toll, toll! heaven is in the sound!
Sad alone to souls unready.
They whose lamps were trimmed and steady
Christ rejoicing found.
On thy rolling waves of tone
Float I to the Master's throne.
Life and love abound.

BELL–SONGS. No. 2.

"Fulgora frango."

SWINGING slowly through the thunder,
Thrill the vivid bolts asunder,
    Make the storm-wind quail.
Hurl thy challenge, stern defender,
Fierce against the tempest's splendor,
    Past the hissing hail.

Leaping through affrighted heaven,
Swift the wrathful flames are driven,
    Flashing death and fear.
Speak, thou bell! with sullen clangor,
Overcry the tempest's anger,
    Force the storm to hear.

Unrelenting, burning, streaming,
Red o'er livid oceans gleaming,
    Lightnings rend the sky.
Break the thunder's fearful chorus,
Lift thy peal of triumph o'er us,
    Floating strong and high.

Tell the soul thy signal story,
How its own inherent glory
    Nature's might shall quell.
Ring a pæan for the spirit
Fire nor flood shall disinherit.
    Praise thy makers, bell!

BELL-SONGS. No. 3.

"Sabbata pango."

CALMLY dawns the golden day,
Over mountains pale and gray.
Man, forsake thy sleep and pray.
Come, come, come!

Swinging through the silent air,
Lo! the call itself is prayer.
Fence thy soul from sin and care.
Come, come, come!

Like a dream, serene and slow,
Through the dawn's aërial glow,
Hear the restful cadence flow:
Come, come, come!

Think that in my pleading tongue,
Through the dewy branches swung,
Christ himself this word hath sung:
Come, come, come!

Toil and battle, rest in peace,
In the holy light's increase,
Weary heart, from labor cease;
    Come, come, come!

Lo! up-rising from the dead,
God's own glory on His head,
His pure lips thy prayers have sped.
    Come, come, come!

THE ICONOCLAST.

A THOUSAND years shall come and go,
  A thousand years of night and day,
And man, through all their changing show,
  His tragic drama still shall play.

Ruled by some fond ideal's power,
  Cheated by passion or despair,
Still shall he waste life's trembling hour,
  In worship vain, and useless prayer.

Ah! where are they who rose in might,
  Who fired the temple and the shrine,
And hurled, through earth's chaotic night,
  The helpless gods it deemed divine?

Cease, longing soul, thy vain desire!
  What idol, in its stainless prime,
But falls, untouched of axe or fire,
  Before the steady eyes of Time.

He looks, and lo! our altars fall,
  The shrine reveals its gilded clay,
With decent hands we spread the pall,
  And, cold with wisdom, glide away.

Oh! where were courage, faith, and truth,
  If man went wandering all his day
In golden clouds of love and youth,
  Nor knew that both his steps betray?

Come, Time, while here we sit and wait,
  Be faithful, spoiler, to thy trust!
No death can further desolate
  The soul that knows its god was dust.

"ALL THY WORKS PRAISE THEE."

I HEAR the distant city-bells
  Clang their loud summons to Thy throne,
Along the wind their music swells,
  And I am here — alone.

The glory of Thy faithful Spring
  Makes for my heart an ardent prayer,
And for my psalm of fervor sing
  The choristers of air.

If any sermonist they need
  Who read Thy word with faithful eyes,
Expositors my spirit feed,
  Inspired from earth and skies.

The life that pours through nature's veins
  Its visible and genial tide,
Thy tender robing of the plains,
  The forest's stately pride ;

The blossom only known to Thee,
  A silent smile that gleams and dies,
The labor-anthem of the bee,
  Whose rest in duty lies;

The solemn chorus of the wind
  That breathes thy power's triumphant tone,—
All frame Thy temple in my mind;
  I am not here alone!

A COMPLAINT.

A HOT noon filled the Autumn sky
So still, the pines forgot to sigh,
But breathed out odors graciously
    Along the slumbering air:
Sweet scents of harvest-gathered grain,
And heavy fruit that wasps profane,
With dead leaves drying on the plain,
    Made silence soft and rare.

There, underneath an evergreen,
Whose boughs against a hill-side lean,
I lingered, wrapt in thoughts serene,
    Half bordering on sleep.
When gently on mine idleness
Stole a low murmur, not distress,
But monotoned to plaintiveness,
    Nor sad enough to weep.

And without thought I had a sense
Of flowers that live in innocence,

Set in the desert's shadow dense,
　　But die, ah me! alone.
Their pale lips breathed, for perfume, song;
Confiding unto speech their wrong,
And, for that I had loved them long,
　　To me they made their moan.

A purple orchis by a brook
Began, — "I see not from my nook
Aught but the summer skies, that look
　　Alike on bud and flower.
Now I am fading, who will know,
With grief that from the earth I go?
Who loved me? still the ripples flow
　　And laugh from hour to hour."

Then a wild-rose complains of death,
That chills the sweetness of her breath,
And more that no clear echo saith
　　To clearer tones, — "Farewell!"
And all the blossoms joined her plaint,
Till the first murmur, sad and faint,
Made in my ear a loud complaint,
　　Yet sweet as chimes a bell.

Then I made answer, — "Beauty grows
For beauty's sake, though no man knows

The hidden place of its repose,
　　It is not vain nor waste.
Dear flowers, for you the wild-birds sing,
Shy fawns behold your blossoming,
And poets, dreaming, at your spring
　　Of visioned sweetness taste.

"And Love that bent the arching sky
Your fair creations satisfy."
Then, sliding into daylight, I
　　Turned my awakened eyes,
And lo! the voice was silent, flowers
Stood round me smiling as the hours,
Content enough with sun and showers,
　　Who mocked me with their cries?

THERE.

"La-bas! la-bas! sous la verdure!"

OH! if I were buried,
Love, thy sweetness could not leave me,
Nor thy smile, false Hope, deceive me,
Neither joy nor terror grieve me
There.

Oh that I were buried!
Grass above mine eyelids growing,
Overhead the wild winds blowing,
Peacefully the slow years flowing,
There.

Oh! if I were buried,
Then my heart were filled forever,
Throbbing pulses cease to quiver,
Cooled in rapture's tranquil river,
There.

Oh that I were buried!
Never any wearied dreaming,
No more night and no more seeming,
Truth's eternal splendor beaming,
There.

Oh! if I were buried,
They who leave me to my sighing,
Would repent above my dying,
But I should not hear their crying
There.

THE DESIRE OF THE MOTH.

GOLDEN-colored miller,
Leave the lamp, and fly away!
In that flame so brightly gleaming,
Sure, though smiling, death is beaming;
Hasten to thy play!

Nearer? foolish miller!
Look! thy tiny wings will burn.
Just escaped, — but soon 'twill reach thee;
Ah! can dying only teach thee
Truths thou wilt not learn?

Didst thou whisper, miller?
Something like a voice and sigh
Seemed to say, — "in all thy teaching,
Is there practice, or but preaching;
Doest thou more than I?"

Wisest little miller!
I indeed have hung too long

Round a flame more wildly burning,
And, with heart too fond and yearning,
Heard no charmer's song.

Blinder than a miller
Hovering with devoted gaze,
Where such visions vain I cherish,
Either they or I must perish,
Like that flickering blaze.

But the moonlight, miller,
Better far befits our mirth;
That calm, streaming light is given
From the silent depths of heaven;
Fire is born of earth!

SEMELE.

"For there bee none of those pagan fables in whiche there lyeth not a more subtle meanynge than the extern expression thereof should att once signifye." — *Marriages of ye Deade.*

SPIRIT of light divine!
  Quick breath of power,
Breathe on these lips of mine,
  Persuade the bud to flower;
Cleave thy dull swathe of cloud! no longer waits the hour.

Exulting, rapturous flame,
  Dispel the night!
I dare not breathe thy name,
  I tremble at thy light,
Yet come! in fatal strength, — come, in all matchless might.

Burn, as the leaping fire
  A martyr's shroud;

Burn, like an Indian pyre,
With music fierce and loud.
Come Power! Love calls thee, — come, with all the god endowed!

Immortal life in death,
On these rapt eyes,
On this quick, failing breath,
In dread and glory rise.
The altar waits thy torch, — come, touch the sacrifice!

Come! not with gifts of life,
Not for my good;
My soul hath kept her strife
In fear and solitude;
More blest the inverted torch, the horror-curdled blood.

Better in light to die
Than silent live;
Rend from these lips one cry,
One death-born utterance give,
Then, clay, in fire depart! then, soul, in heaven survive!

RECORDARE.

M.

Even as the Summer cries,
When the sunshine southward flies,
Weeping, weeping silently,
So I sit and mourn for thee.

Dreams that to thy dwelling go,
And come home alone and slow,
Constant springs of sorrow be,
As I sit and mourn for thee.

I remember all thy ways,
Sweeter than my lips can praise;
All I give that memory,
Is to sit and mourn for thee.

How should angels longer spare
One on earth without compare?
Thou, to their dear company,—
I, to sit and mourn for thee.

For the living be the moan.
Widowed, motherless, alone,
Love! alone for them and me,
Here I sit and mourn for thee.

Cradled in divine repose,
Thy new life of rapture flows.
God be thanked! too blest to see
How I sit and mourn for thee!

THE RIVER.

The river flows and flows away,
A lonely stream through forests gray,
No rippled rapids o'er it play;
  Forever and forever.
As silent as a winter's night,
With purple heavens all alight,
And planets shining strangely bright;
  So quiet is the river.

No fount nor fall the vision finds,
And in no devious course it winds,
But straight from where the sunset shines,
  Forever and forever.
A mystery of shade and gleam,
O'er hidden rocks glides on the stream,
Like sleep above a fearful dream;
  So quiet is the river.

It streams pure silver in the sun,
Slow, sullen lead, with storms begun,
And golden green when day is done,
  Forever and forever.

A flow of pearl in moonlight cold,
With moonless midnight onward rolled,
Blacker than Lethe streamed of old.
  So quiet is the river.

Oh, water! by thy waves serene,
As tranquil hours a life hath seen,
No more to be as they have been
  Forever and forever.
For underneath its restless flow,
Too black for light's full noon to show,
Lie broken rocks no mortals know.
  So quiet is the river.

SONG.

Airs of Summer that softly blow,
Sing your whispering songs to me,
Over the grass like a shadow go,
Flutter your wings in the rustling tree.

Curl the wave on the sunny sand,
Rock the bee in its rose asleep,
Scatter odors from strand to strand,
Over ocean in laughter sweep.

Kiss the snows on the mountain height,
Vex the river that leaps beneath,
Sing in the fir-trees your sweet good-night,
And cease like a baby's slumbering breath.

EN ESPAGNE.

I BUILT a Palace, white and high,
With sweeping purple tapestried;
No dusty highway ran thereby,
But guarded alleys to it led;
And shaven lawns about were spread,
Where bird and moth danced daintily.

So gracious were its portals wide,
So light and fair the turrets stood,
No flaw mine eager eye espied,
I fashioned it, and called it good;
And lavished on its solitude
All garnishings of pomp and pride.

That was in golden summer-time;—
The winter-wind is howling now,
My Palace has passed out of time,—
The sward is only sheeted snow,
Its hangings with the dead leaves blow:
There comes an end to mortal prime.

And I, who laid it stone by stone,
Stone after stone do take it down.
What if a king, whose state had flown,
Should pull apart his regal crown?
For kingly hearts no fate can frown,
They rule forever o'er their own.

LA COQUETTE.

You look at me with tender eyes,
That, had you worn a month ago,
Had slain me with divine surprise:—
But now I do not see them glow.

I laugh to hear your laughter take
A softer thrill, a doubtful tone,—
I know you do it for my sake.
You rob the nest whose bird is flown.

Not twice a fool, if twice a child!
I know you now, and care no more
For any lie you may have smiled,
Than that starved beggar at your door.

He has the remnants of your feast;
You offer me your wasted heart!
He may enact the welcome guest;
I shake the dust off and depart.

If you had known a woman's grace
And pitied me who died for you,
I could not look you in the face,
When now you tell me you are "true."

True! — If the fallen seraphs wear
A lovelier face of false surprise
Than you at my unmoving air,
There is no truth this side the skies.

But this *is* true, that once I loved. —
You scorned and laughed to see me die;
And now you think the heart so proved
Beneath your feet again shall lie!

I had the pain when you had power;
Now mine the power, who reaps the pain?
You sowed the wind in that black hour;
Receive the whirlwind for your gain!

OCTOBER.

"Rest! rest! shall I not have all Eternity to rest in?" — ARNAULD.

THERE comes a time of rest to thee,
Whose laden boughs droop heavily
Toward earth, thou golden-fruited tree!

A time when wind and tempest cease
To spoil and stain thy fair increase:
After fruition deepest peace.

The tender bloom that decked thee, bride,
The jewels of thy matron pride,
And purple robes, — all laid aside.

The slow, red sunshine, o'er thee cast,
In sweet, sad kisses for thy last,
And shadow-haunted from the past.

Green, leafy, quiet, freed from care,
No heavier weight thy lithe limbs bear
Than dripping rain and sunny air.

But unto man's diviner sense
The strenuous rest of penitence
Remaineth only for defence.

His fruit drops slowly from his hands,
But only with the dropping sands
That fall on Time's slow-gathering strands.

The sower in this mortal field
Shall reap no harvest's gracious yield,
The warrior conquers — on his shield.

But after life and fruit and rest,
Thou, tree! by dust shalt be possessed;
To him remains a day more blest,

A newer hope, a summer-time
Renewed forever in its prime,
Where God, his harvest, sits sublime.

LOSS AND GAIN.

HOPE went singing southward,
And left me silent here;
I did not scorn nor sorrow,
I had no smile nor tear;
For out of the door beside her,
Went her serving-maiden, Fear.

Where there comes no morning,
There never is any night;
The clouds will fly from heaven
When the sun shall lose its light;
And he who wants the pleasure
Wants the pain of sight.

Rain and rainbow vanish,
But the sky is undismayed;
Hope and Fear may leave us,
And the price of life be paid;
Greater than any passion
Is the soul that God hath made.

Go! walk the world together,
And trouble the hearts of men;
Go paint and pluck the blossoms
That never shall bloom again;
But dread the day of Heaven:
Ye both shall perish then!

"NON FIT."

THE poet's thoughts are full of might,
Elate with glory and delight;
New tints are in his heavens spread;
On odors keen his sense is fed,
And strains accordant angels sing;
Through all his sleep their echoes ring.

The poet has a lonely soul;
He hears the seas in thunder roll,
Perceives the rapture of the rose,
And every tone of Nature knows;
But cannot speak the tongue of men,
Or give their greetings back again.

His eyes alight with love intense,
His face all calm with innocence;
The green leaves kiss his waving hair,
The wild-birds sing him carols rare,
Intent to celebrate and bless;
His Eden fills the wilderness.

But all his songs are minor-keyed;
His prayers are less to praise than plead,
His smiles are full of grief asleep,
His heart like ocean's bitter deep;
For tears and laughter, hand in hand,
About his vibrant nature stand.

At this the world admiring gaze,
And think they feed his soul with praise;
But whisper in a loud aside,
"Is this your poet's vaunted pride?
Why, better be the common clay
Than thus 'twixt heaven and hell astray."

But he, respiring sudden fire,
Hears and replies in righteous ire,
"Better to sound the depths of hell,
If thence to heaven our praises swell;
Nobler than life, or love, to die
Transfixed with immortality!"

SEPTEMBER.

SORROWFUL Autumn! my summer is over;
  Roses no longer shall surfeit the bee;
White crowding daisies and honey-sweet clover
  Shiver and perish, breathed on by thee.

All the fair blossoms that trembled at morning,
  Heavy with dew in the wandering wind,
Hang their frail bells at thy trumpet of warning,
  Scatter their lives on the tempest unkind.

Over the forest the bitterns are flying,
  Golden and scarlet the maple-trees stand,
Out of the black East a rain-song is sighing,
  Pitiless, desolate, death is at hand!

Far in the North, like a vision of sorrow,
  Rise the white snow-drifts to topple and fall;
Winds of wild fury shall hurl them to-morrow
  Deeply and hopelessly far over all.

Ah! what new Spring shall awaken the glory
  Vanished forever in darkness to-day?
Falser than fair is Hope's eloquent story,
  Roses once withered are withered for aye.

THE LOST ANCHOR.

THERE lies a rusted anchor
  Deep in the white sea-sand;
Where trails the good ship's cable
  That parted, strand by strand?

The north-wind roared and thundered,
  The leaping waves ran high;
Dark on the foaming water
  Shut down the stormy sky.

But still the lithe mast quivered
  Under the flapping sail;
The cordage shrieked and rattled,
  And yelled the furious gale.

One strain — one plunge — one struggle —
  The mighty strands give way —
Now far from home and harbor,
  Away, away, away!

Beyond the sight of shelter,
  Far out her stern-lights shine.
Poor ship, to lose thine anchor,
  Poor broken hope of mine !

THEN.

I give thee treasures hour by hour,
  That old-time princes asked in vain,
And pined for in their useless power,
  Or died of passion's eager pain.

I give thee love as God gives light,
  Aside from merit or from prayer,
Rejoicing in its own delight,
  And freer than the lavish air.

I give thee prayers like jewels strung
  On golden threads of hope and fear,
And tenderer thoughts than ever hung
  In a sad angel's pitying tear.

As earth pours freely to the sea
  Its thousand streams of wealth untold,
So flows my silent life to thee,
  Glad that its very sands are gold.

What care I for thy carelessness?
  I give from depths that overflow;
Regardless that their power to bless
  Thy spirit cannot sound or know.

Far lingering on a distant dawn,
  My triumph shines, more sweet than late,
When, from these mortal mists withdrawn,
  Thine heart shall know me. — I can wait.

FANTASIA.

When I am a sea-flower
Under the cool green tide,
Where the sunshine slants and quivers,
And the quaint, gray fishes glide,
I'll shut and sleep at noonday,
At night on the waves I'll ride,
And see the surf in moonshine
Rush on the black rocks' side.

When I am a sea-bird,
Under the clouds I'll fly,
And 'light on a rocking billow
Tossing low and high.
Safe from the lee-shore's thunder,
Mocking the mariner's cry,
Drifting away on the tempest,
A speck on the sullen sky!

When I am a sea-wind,
I'll watch for a ship I know,

Through the sails and rigging
Merrily I will blow.
The crew shall be like dead men
White with horror and woe;
Then I'll sing like a spirit,
And let the good ship go.

SONG.

Night comes creeping slowly o'er me,
  Like a vapor cold and gray;
Dim the track that lies before me,
  Lost the lingering smile of day.

As a river, nearing ocean,
  Drops the brooklet's merry bell,
I forget hope's wild emotion;
  Love and life, farewell, farewell!

Eyes above me raining sorrow,
  Lips too tender to be true,
In the sunshine of to-morrow
  Glow and sweetness shall renew.

I have trod a weary measure,
  Fairy-tales no more I tell.
False is pain, and fleeting pleasure;
  Love and life, farewell, farewell!

Softly through the darkened heaven,
  Like a vision in the night,
Float the purple wings of even;
  No more laughter, no more light.

Close mine eyes, worn out with weeping,
  Weary pulses rest as well!
In the dust and silence sleeping,
  Love and life, farewell, farewell!

BIRD MUSIC.

SINGER of priceless melody,
Unguerdoned chorister of air,
Who from the lithe top of the tree
Pourest at will thy music rare,
As if a sudden brook laughed down the hill-side there.

The purple-blossomed fields of grass,
Waved sea-like to the idle wind,
Thick daisies that the stars surpass,
Being as fair and far more kind;—
All sweet uncultured things thy wild notes bring to mind.

When that enraptured overflow
Of singing into silence dies,
Thy rapid fleeting pinions show
Where all thy spell of sweetness lies
Gathered in one small nest from the wide earth and skies.

Unconscious of thine audience,
  Careless of praises as of blame,
In simpleness and innocence,
  Thy gentle life pursues its aim,
So tender and serene, that we might blush for
    shame.

The patience of thy brooding wings
  That droop in silence day by day,
The little crowd of callow things
  That joy for weariness repay,—
These are the living spring, thy song the fountain's
    spray.

FASTRADA'S RING.

"Stretch out thy hand, insatiate Time!
  Keeper of keys, restore to me
Some gift that in the gray Earth's prime
  Her happy children held of thee;
Some signet of that mystery
  Thy footsteps trample into death,
Some score of that strange harmony
  That sings in every breath."

So sung I on an autumn-day,
  Sitting in silence, golden, clear,
When even the mild winds seemed to pray
  Beside the slowly dying year,
And the old conqueror stopped to hear;
  For, like the echo of a bell,
I heard him speak, in accents clear:
  "Choose! and thy wise choice tell!"

Then all my vanishing desires,
  The threads of hope and joy and pain,

Long burned in life's consuming fires,
  Came glittering into life again,
And, gathered as a summer rain
  Into the rainbow's bended wing,
Cried, with one voice of longing vain:
  "Give me Fastrada's ring!

"Give me that talisman of peace
  She wore upon her finger white,
Then shall the weary visions cease,
  That haunt me all the lingering night;
The world shall blossom with delight,
  And birds of heaven about me sing;
Ah! fill these darkened eyes with light!
  Give me Fastrada's ring!

"Give me no jewels from thy store,
  No learned scrolls, no gems of art;
My eager wishes grasp at more:
  Sleep for a worn and wretched heart;
A draught to melt these lips apart,
  Sealed with such thirst as death-pains bring;
Love, — life's sole rest and better part,
  Give me Fastrada's ring!"

TRUTHS.

I WEAR a rose in my hair,
Because I feel like a weed;
Who knows that the rose is thorny
And makes my temples bleed?
If one gets to his journey's end, what matter how galled the steed?

I gloss my face with laughter,
Because I cannot be calm;
When you listen to the organ,
Do you hear the words of the psalm?
If they give you poison to drink, 'tis better to call it balm.

If I sneer at youth's wild passion,
Who fancies I break my heart?
'Tis this world's righteous fashion,
With a sneer to cover a smart.
Better to give up living than not to play your part.

If I scatter gold like a goblin,
My life may yet be poor.
Does Love come in at the window
When Money stands at the door?
I am what I seem to men. Need I be any more?

God sees from the high blue heaven,
He sees the grape in the flower;
He hears one's life-blood dripping
Through the maddest, merriest hour;
He knows what sackcloth and ashes hide in the purple of power.

The broken wing of the swallow
He binds in the middle air;
I shall be what I am in Paradise —
So, heart, no more despair!
Remember the blessed Jesus, and wipe his feet with thy hair.

MY RED CARNATION.

S. C. W.

Redder than any summer-rose,
Far redder than the garnet glows,
And set beside the lily's snows,
  Fair blossom, bloom for me!
With Indian breath of sun-kissed spice,
And dainty petals, point-device,
What florist ever knew thy price,
  Or half thy charms could see?

As tropic in thy breathing glow,
As if Asiatic winds did blow
Thy crown of beauty to and fro,
  And sway thy slender stem;
Yet statelier in floral pride
Than any queen that flaunts a bride,
Such quaint and courtly graces glide
  Around thy diadem.

Thy leaf should point its verdant lance
By castle-walls of old romance,
Where fountains to the soft airs dance,
  And glittering peacocks trail;
Or white swans break the sullen sleep
Of some old lake, set dark and deep
Among the trees that o'er it weep
  When autumn eves grow pale.

The violet hath a fond perfume,
The passion-flower a mystic bloom,
And heather spreads its cloud of gloom
  O'er highland mountains bare;
The red rose veils a heart of flame,
And blushes with unconscious shame,
The snow-drop fits its icy name,
  Most frigid and most fair.

But thou art love that pride adorns
The rose's heart without its thorns,
A child of summer's fragrant morns,
  Dew-christened by the night.
Ah! cold and fair to others be,
But spread thy glowing heart to me,
And, as thou wert, still ever be
  My darling and delight.

There's never a tided ocean
  Without a shore;
Nor a leaf whose downward motion
  No dews deplore;
And I dream that my devotion
  May move thee to sigh once more.

DEPARTING.

Weep not for the dead! they lie
Safe from every changing sky;
Over them thou shalt not cry
        Any more.
Weep for him whose lessening sail,
Borne upon an outward gale,
Sees the beacon faint and fail
        On the shore.

Weep not for the dead: they sleep
Where no evil visions creep;
God hath sealed their slumber deep
        Till His day.
Weep for him who fleeth fast
On a fierce and alien blast,
Torn from all the haunted past,
        Far away.

He shall never see again
Home-lit valley, hill, or plain;

He shall mourn and cry in vain
O'er the dead.
Wandering in a stranger-land,
None shall grasp his listless hand,
No sweet sister-nurse shall stand
By his bed.

Weep for him, and weep for those
Who shall never more unclose
Home's dear portals, nor repose
In its rest.
Foreign where their kindred dwell,
Strange where they have loved too well,
Homesick as no speech can tell,
All unblest.

For the dead thou shalt not mourn,
He hath reached a peaceful bourne;
Weep for him, the travel-worn,
All alone!
Life's long torture he must bear
Till his very soul despair,
Helpless both for cry or prayer;
Make his moan!

A STATUE.

DREAM divine and tender,
  Frozen into stone;
Pall nor purple splendor
  Round thy grace is thrown;
Thou standest like a star, clothed in thy light alone.

Silent with the passion
  Of thy new despair;
In the spotless fashion
  That all angels wear;
Like softly falling snow thy presence fills the air.

On thy lips half-parted,
  Sleeps a dreaming sigh;
Love and hope departed
  Droop thy pensive eye;
And anguish on thy brow hath set her majesty.

Neither shame nor madness
  Touch thy spirit pure;

A STATUE.

Dream divine and tender,
  Frozen into stone;
Pall nor purple splendor
  Round thy grace is thrown;
Thou standest like a star, clothed in thy light alone.

Silent with the passion
  Of thy new despair;
In the spotless fashion
  That all angels wear;
Like softly falling snow thy presence fills the air.

On thy lips half-parted,
  Sleeps a dreaming sigh;
Love and hope departed
  Droop thy pensive eye;
And anguish on thy brow hath set her majesty.

Neither shame nor madness
  Touch thy spirit pure;

Regally hath sadness
  Taught thee to endure;
Earth passes at thy feet, but heaven is ever sure.

Like the languid tolling
  Of a funeral bell,
Or the awful rolling
  Of the ocean's swell,
Thou stillest sound with awe, through power's sublimest spell.

In what holy vision
  Of a midnight moon,
Did thy shape Elysian
  Rise, like some sad tune,
Through the rapt sculptor's soul, and turn his night to noon?

Utter thus forever,
  With resistless tongue,
Higher thought than ever
  Bird or breeze hath sung;
For Beauty never dies, and Grace is ever young.

A PICTURE.

UPON her pale cheek, day by day,
No tender, rosy blushes play ;
The shadows gathered on her hair
Lie soft above her forehead fair ;
    A frailer shade is she.

No footstep on the stone goes by,
But strikes a fire across her eye;
No sudden voice a word can speak,
But flashes red light on her cheek;
    Such guards her quick thoughts be.

All day she sees the sullen rain
Splash slow against the window-pane;
All night the south-wind makes its moan,
About her chamber low and lone ;
    She cannot die nor rest.

Like some old saint in cell withdrawn,
In prayer and penance till the dawn,

So her sad soul its vigil holds,
As year on year to life unfolds,
    And wears her patient breast.

Not any leech can find a cure
For these slow miseries that endure,
Till heaven before her eyes shall ope
The golden gate foreseen by hope,
    And medicine her heart.

There is no new life for the dead,
No gathering up the tears once shed;
Pray, ye beloved, who pity her,
That God no more that rest defer;
    Pray that her soul depart.

ROSEMARY.

EARTH'S singing time and floral weather,
With golden flower and scarlet feather,
Have vanished in the South together,
    And left me with the frost.
Where thrush and oriole hovered brightly,
The sparrows hop and twitter lightly,
And crows fly from the sea-ward nightly,
    By hurried north-winds tossed.

Gray storm-clouds in the dark east lying,
Through leafless woods the crickets crying,
And toward the happy tropics flying,
    A line of silent birds.
All these have tales of drear November,
And bid me, shivering, here remember
Long nights when redly burns the ember,
    And fast fly eager words.

Forever past are songs and roses,
The Summer deep in leaves reposes,

And life has done with tuneful closes,
    Now let the ashes sleep.
For us whose summer hymn is ending,
Its chorus with sweet echoes blending,
Shall still be on and upward tending,
    Till eyes no more can weep.

Another Spring its censers swinging,
Shall wake again both bloom and singing,
And wild brooks from their dumbness springing,
    Go chattering down the hills.
What if the dust beside them sleeping,
Last year had laughter, life, and weeping?
Earth drops such memories from her keeping,
    To-day her whole heart fills.

Now withered leaves fall in the grasses,
While rain and wind sing funeral masses,
And like a veil the dank mist passes
    Across the bleak world's face.
This dreary time is fit for sorrow,
But love and hope good cheer can borrow,
And while we die, they wait the morrow
    Their sunshine to replace.

WOOD LAUREL.

Queen regnant of the summer wood,
That hearest thrush and hangbird cry,
With such a dream-like majesty
As crowns thee, out of solitude,
The fairest flower that ever stood,
Impassive, safe from sympathy.

Light roseate cloud of dawning day,
Hung floating in the gloom of leaves,
Vainly for thee the night-wind grieves,
Vainly all forest-murmurs stray.
In thy cold blossoms vainly play
The thousand love-songs Nature weaves.

So pure, so perfect, so serene,
With tender, mocking blushes dyed,
The cankerous honey-dew of pride,
Charms soft and deadly in thy mien,
The natural sceptre of a queen,
Heart frozen, but half deified.

Beware, oh glancing butterfly!
The rosy bloom is sweet to see,
But have thou care of majesty,
The serf that loves the queen must die.
Gay, living blossom! dance and fly
To humbler feasts, secure for thee.

Assiduous honey-bee, beware!
Those bright cups glow with poisoned wine;
The wild-rose and the columbine
Have simple treasures, safe to share.
This regal beauty holds thy snare,
The form, but not the soul, divine.

NEMESIS.

WITH eager steps I go
Across the valleys low,
Where in deep brakes the writhing serpents hiss.
Above, below, around,
I hear the dreadful sound
Of thy calm breath, eternal Nemesis!

Over the mountains high,
Where silent snow-drifts lie,
And greet the red morn with a pallid kiss,
There, in the awful night,
I see the solemn light
Of thy clear eyes, avenging Nemesis!

Far down in lonely caves,
Dark as the empty graves
That wait our dead hopes and our perished bliss,
Though to their depths I flee,
Still do my fixed eyes see
Thy pendant sword, unchanging Nemesis!

Inevitable fate!
Still must thy phantoms wait.
And mock my shadow like its fearful twin?
Is there no final rest
In this doom-haunted breast?
Does thy terrific patience wait therein?

"Aye! wander as thou wilt,
The blood thy hand hath spilt
Stamps on thy brow its black, eternal sign;
Thyself thou canst not flee.
Writhe in thine agony!
Suffer! despair! thou art condemned—and mine."

"CREDE TANTUM."

DEAR weeper at the grassy bed,
  Where Love lies cold, with folded eyes,
The life thou mournest is not dead,
  Wait, and have faith, it shall arise!

If, from thy narrow dell of earth,
  It seems for some new heaven to soar;
Distrust not Love's immortal birth,
  Believe it lives, to die no more.

Have faith! have faith! though cold and death
  Dim the soft eye and still the heart,
Though closed the lips and hushed the breath,
  Though hope and fear alike depart.

Believe, for surer than the rise
  Of morning o'er the stagnant sea,
New light shall fill those frozen eyes,
  New smiles shall part thy lips for thee.

Love never dies: it cannot die;
  Nor flood, nor fire, nor rending heaven,
Can make the heart its life deny,
  Or gather back the gift once given.

There comes a Spring for every snow,
  For every death a life hereafter;
And they whose tears have bitterest flow,
  Shall fill their lips with sweetest laughter.

THE FISHING SONG.

DOWN in the wide, gray river,
  The current is sweeping strong;
Over the wide, gray river,
  Floats the fisherman's song.

The oar-stroke times the singing;
  The song falls with the oar;
And an echo in both is ringing;
  I thought to hear no more.

Out of a deeper current,
  The song brings back to me
A cry from mortal silence,
  Of mortal agony.

Life that was spent and vanished,
  Love that had died of wrong,
Hearts that are dead in living,
  Come back on the fisherman's song.

I see the maples leafing,
  Just as they leafed before;
The green grass comes no greener
  Down to the very shore.

And the rude song swelling, sinking,
  In the cadence of days gone by,
As the oar, from the water drinking,
  Ripples the mirrored sky.

Yet the soul hath life diviner;
  Its past returns no more;
But in echoes that answer the minor
  Of the boat-song from the shore.

And the ways of God are darkness,
  His judgment waiteth long;
He breaks the heart of a woman
  With a fisherman's careless song.

JULY XXIV.

Come back! come back! forsake thy rest,
  And tread the darkened paths of men!
Bring gladness to the lonely breast,
  Peace to the troubled dreams again.

Nor yet without a ransom, Death,
  I plead to loose thy dread embrace!
I offer thee but breath for breath,
  Give this one life to fill my place.

For thee, lost sleeper, tears are shed
  That fall not for the slave set free;
Thou, mourned as those too early dead;
  I, mourning in captivity.

For thee the life-rose, blooming, glowed;
  I long perceive its naked thorn;
For thee, soft spread the widening road
  I see grow narrower every morn.

Send the keen rapture of surprise,
  A sudden joy through silent hearts,
And shut a smile within mine eyes,
  Like one who for his home departs.

Come back! come back! the love and grief,
  Poured on thy sleep, may yet be mine,
As late dews mourn the fallen leaf,
  That on its sunlight would not shine.

HESPER.

SUNSET on the mountains hoary,
    Deepens into night;
Day hath lost its crown of glory,
    Life hath lost its light.

In mine eyes the tears are springing,
    For thy face I see;
In my heart its dreams are singing,
    Mournful songs of thee.

All the sunshine fled from heaven
    With thy closing eyes;
Yet on me, at lonely even,
    Clear as stars they rise.

Though the way be long and dreary
    Down the mountain's side,
I no more can call it weary,
    Thou art there my bride!

I behold thy garments flowing,
    Snow-like, in the moon;
See thy parted lips are glowing,
    Red as flowers in June.

Underneath the daisies lying,
    Lost in dreamless sleep;
Thou hast heard my nightly crying,
    Thou hast left my sleep.

All the night in visions tender,
    Love and life return;
Until morning's cloudy splendor
    O'er the hills shall burn.

Day glides slowly o'er the meadow,
    Love and life to steal;
But the first star's trembling shadow
    Brings a bridal peal.

RÊVE DU MIDI.

WHEN o'er the mountain steeps
The hazy noontide creeps,
And the shrill cricket sleeps
  Under the grass;
When soft the shadows lie,
And clouds sail o'er the sky,
And the idle winds go by,
With the heavy scent of blossoms as they pass;

Then, when the silent stream
Lapses as in a dream,
And the water-lilies gleam
  Up to the sun;
When the hot and burdened day
Stops on its downward way,
When the moth forgets to play,
And the plodding ant may dream her toil is done;

Then, from the noise of war,
And the din of earth afar,
Like some forgotten star

Dropt from the sky;
With the sounds of love and fear,
All voices sad and dear
Banish to silence drear,
The willing thrall of trances sweet I lie.

Some melancholy gale
Breathes its mysterious tale,
Till the rose's lips grow pale
With her sighs:
And o'er my thoughts are cast
Tints of the vanished past,
Glories that faded fast,
Renewed to splendour in my dreaming eyes.

As poised on vibrant wings,
Where his sweet treasure swings,
The honey-lover clings
To the red flowers:
So, lost in vivid light,
So, rapt from day and night,
I linger in delight,
Enraptured o'er the vision-freighted hours.

TWILIGHT.

ALONE I watch the setting sun
  Brighten the hill-tops in the west,
And clouds that on the swift winds run
  To gather splendour o'er his rest.

Oh! had I but those wings of air,
  Across the mountain heights to flee!
Thine eyes should lose their shade of care,
  Thy weary face grow bright for me.

Or could I capture sparks of fire,
  To do the message of my thought,
Their joyful speed no space should tire,
  Till love and light for thee they brought.

But darker, deeper, grows the night,
  And my sad thoughts more restless far;
I would I were a ray of light
  To greet thee from yon lonely star.

Dear star! watch gently from on high,
  What my frail vision cannot see;
A gentler and more powerful eye,
  Shines through thy tender gleam for me.

One heart, o'er mountains, through the night,
  Protects and loves, while I despair;
He turns the depths of gloom to light,
  And gives my wishes wings of prayer.

DAISIES.

FAIR and peaceful daisies,
  Smiling in the grass,
Who hath sung your praises?
  Poets by you pass,
And I alone am left to celebrate your mass.

In the summer morning,
  Through the fields ye shine,
Joyfully adorning
  Earth with grace divine,
And pour, from sunny hearts, fresh gladness into mine.

Lying in the meadows,
  Like the milky way,
From nocturnal shadows
  Glad to fall away,
And live a happy life in the wide light of day.

Bees about you humming
  Pile their yellow store,

Winds in whispers coming
  Teach you love's sweet lore,
For your reluctant lips still worshipping the more.

Birds with music laden
  Shower their songs on you;
And the rustic maiden,
  Standing in the dew,
By your alternate leaves tells if her love be true.

Little stars of glory!
  From your amber eyes
No inconstant story
  Of her love should rise!
And yet "He loves me not!" is oft the sad surprise.

Crowds of milk-white blossoms!
  Noon's concentred beams
Glowing in your bosoms;
  So, by living streams
In heaven, I think the light of flowers immortal gleams.

When your date is over,
  Peacefully ye fade,

With the fragrant clover
  And sweet grasses laid,
In odors for a pall beneath the orchard shade.

Happy, happy daisies!
  Would I were like you,
Pure from human praises,
  Fresh with morning dew,
And ever in my heart to heaven's clear sunshine true!

CHAMOMILE.

Now heart! send forth thy sweetness!
  Crushed, — trampled in the dust, —
  Remember God is just:
And for man's incompleteness
Let the soft incense of thy pity rise:
Make a burnt-offering of the sacrifice!

Think, in thy bitter anguish,
  Thou hast not done the wrong, —
  This echo of a song
Whose faint, sad minors languish
Against thy will or care, shall comfort thee,
Wouldst thou the wounded or the weapon be?

Art thou too weak and weary,
  Too pitiless in pain,
  To love where love is vain?
Waste starlight on the dreary,
The self-lost, and the cold? for such is one
For whom thy vernal life is all undone.

The spring-forsaken blossom,
Drooping its pallid leaves,
Not without purpose grieves;
For hidden in its bosom
Lies the green fruit, — have patience, trust, and truth;
God keeps the sunshine of thy darkened youth.

Sore, bruised, and bleeding
Under the cruel tread,
Let thy pure odors spread,
And up to heaven pleading,
Draw showered forgiveness on the heart of stone,
More pitiful than thine, because far more alone.

RIGHTS.

I HEARD a voice cry through the night,
Crying from off some lonely height,
A gently earnest cry for Right.

Through the sad sweetness of that voice
A stifled echo did rejoice,
As if the sadness were of choice.

And all along the south-wind spread,
With scents and dews its tones were shed,
Shadowed with vagueness, not with dread.

But gathering more articulate,
Breathless I heard soft lips relate
The grievance of their mortal state.

"I will have Right! my right to be
First in all love-borne ministry;
The spring beneath thy roots, O tree!

"My right, when toiling and dismay
Oppress the burdened noon of day,
To freshen it with salt sea-spray.

"To be, when hearts shall fail for fear,
Seeing eclipse of suns draw near,
A star-shine in the darkness clear.

"To be, in this world-beaten dust,
A still evangelist of trust,
Waving white wings before the just.

"My right to stand beside the dead,
With hands upon the living head,
Both unto rest eternal led.

"My right to pure child-tears and smiles,
To baby-love and tender wiles,
Hope, that the weariest heart beguiles.

"I will not have thy place, O man!
By petronel and barbican,
Or reeking in the battle's van.

"My strength against the ruder foe,
I will be thine beneath the blow,
My right to love, and thine to know."

"YOURS EVER."

No more, no more! the words are vain;
  No longer mine, and ne'er to be:
The dead heart cannot live again,
  The stream run upward from the sea.

The past is past, forever fled:
  I lost thee on a weary day,
My life's one prayer was backward read,
  My soul's last refuge torn away.

Not mine, not mine! no, never mine.
  What years shall gather to their bough
The sere leaves of the blasted pine?
  Think what I was! — what am I now?

Not God, nor I, had rent apart
  Thy tender clasp of living love;
Thine own hand tore the trembling heart,
  That vainly prayed, and vainly strove.

No, never mine! all angels keep
  Their faithful watch about thy way,
Around thy steps, above thy sleep!
  To God I give thee while I may.

Forever His, but never mine.
  Ah! when this fearful life shall flee,
Wrapt safely in His rest divine,
  I shall not even lament for thee!

PRAYER.

Oh, Love divine, ineffable!
  Help the weak heart that strays from thee!
And battling with the hosts of hell,
  Doubts or despairs of victory:
  For Thou hast died upon the tree,
Thine anguish poured in bloody sweat,
And can thy yearning heart forget
  The first-fruits of that agony?
  O Lord, in glory, think on me!

Thy tenderness no mother knows,
  Not she who sees her darling pine,
And weeps that dying shadows close
  Above the lamb she knows is thine;
  But Thou, my God, art all divine!
Thy banished shall return again;
Thy life poured out like summer rain —
  Those dying pangs exchanged for mine —
  Are not an alien's birth-right sign.

I know that from the depths of sin,
  The uttermost abyss of woe,
Thine arm my trembling soul shall win,
  Thy piercing eyes thy child shall know.
  Though mortal love forget to flow —
Though mortal faith grow cold and die —
Thy love is called eternity,
  Thy truth is morning's orient glow,
  And wide as space shall ever grow.

Come, prince of darkness, with thy bands!
  Their leaguered host a child defies,
For He who holds me in his hands
  Shall like a stern avenger rise,
  And turn on thee those heavenly eyes
That tears of pity shed for me;
But burn with judgment over thee
  And those who dare his love despise, —
  Then stoop and bear me to the skies.

VI ET ARMIS.

My soul be strong! confront thy life,
Nor feebly moan with weak complaint;
Arouse to wage the mortal strife,
Thou shrinking coward, pale and faint!

Look up at truth's unchanging face;
That brow, though stern, is yet serene;
And sometimes, for the heart of grace,
On those calm lips a smile hath been.

The warrior on the battle-field
Lingers no more to look behind,
But raises high his bossy shield,
And casts his banner to the wind.

It will not serve thee to delay;
Shall the wide ocean cease to roar,
Because thy wild and dangerous way
Lies to its dimly visioned shore?

Shake off thy dreams; let faith and prayer
 Light the drear way: thy path is strait,
Contagion fills the misty air,
 And clustering snares around thee wait.

Hope not for succor from below!
 Stars shine from heaven, but shine at night.
Be stout of heart, come weal or woe;
 Forward, — and God defend the Right!

PSYCHE TO EROS.

SURVIVE, O Love, this sad estate;
  Why shouldst thou with the sunshine fly?
Hast thou no more enduring date
  Than out of one despair to die?
The fiercest tempest only brings
At worst a drenching to thy wings.

Thou art not such a mortal thing,
  That any agonies of pain,
Which from thy trampled offerings spring,
  Can crush thee into dust again.
Look with clear eyes, and lift thy head,
Bruised, wounded, bleeding, but not dead.

Not dead, — there lives no mortal hand,
  However mighty, strong as thou;
No human malice ever planned
  A shadow that could soil thy brow.
Crowned with thy sure divinity,
Arise and reign; the shadows flee!

INDOLENCE.

INDOLENT, indolent! yes, I am indolent;
  So is the grass growing tenderly, slowly;
  So is the violet fragrant and lowly,
Drinking in quietness, peace, and content;
  So is the bird on the light branches swinging,
  Idly his carol of gratitude singing,
Only on living and loving intent.

Indolent, indolent! yes, I am indolent;
  So is the cloud overhanging the mountain;
  So is the tremulous wave of a fountain,
Uttering softly its silvery psalm.
  Nerve and sensation in quiet reposing,
  Silent as blossoms the night-dew is closing,
But the full heart beating strongly and calm.

Indolent, indolent! yes, I am indolent,
  If it be idle to gather my pleasure
  Out of creation's uncoveted treasure,
Midnight and morning, by forest and sea,

Wild with the tempest's sublime exultation,
  Lonely in Autumn's forlorn lamentation,
Hopeful and happy with Spring and the bee.

Indolent, indolent! are ye not indolent?
  Thralls of the earth and its usages weary,
  Toiling like gnomes where the darkness is dreary,
Toiling and sinning to heap up your gold!
  Stifling the heavenward breath of devotion,
  Crushing the freshness of every emotion;
Hearts like the dead which are pulseless and cold!

Indolent, indolent! art thou not indolent?
  Thou who art living unloving and lonely,
  Wrapped in a pall that will cover thee only,
Shrouded in selfishness, piteous ghost!
  Sad eyes behold thee, and angels are weeping
  O'er thy forsaken and desolate sleeping;
Art thou not indolent? art thou not lost?

NOCTURN.

I.

Night hovering o'er the languid lily-bell,
Pours shade and sleep;
Dim loitering brooks their dripping rosaries tell;
And shadows creep,
Like ghosts that haunt a dream, through forests still
and deep.

Cool odors sigh across the rustling leaves
In dew distilled;
Far through the hills some falling river grieves;
All earth is stilled,
Save where a dreaming bird with sudden song is
thrilled.

The sunshine, tangled in the chestnut boughs,
In darkness dies;
Flowers, with shut eyelids, pay their peaceful vows,
And daylight lies
Faint in the fading West to see the stars arise.

Sleep, weary soul! the folding arms of night
For thee are spread;
Her fresh, cool kisses on thy brow alight;
Droop, aching head!
Receive the slumberous dew these gracious heavens have shed.

Thy day is long, thy noontide hot and sere;
But eve hath come
To sing low anthems in thy trancèd ear
Like welcomes home,
And prelude this brief sleep with songs of one to come.

NOCTURN.

II.

DEAR night, from the hills return!
Darkness hath passed away,
And I see the flush of morning burn,
Red o'er the mountains gray.
My life is like a song
That a bird sings in its sleeping,
Or a hidden stream that flows along
To the sound of its own soft weeping.

Sunlight is made for care,
For the weary languid day;
When the locust cymbals beat the air,
And the hot winds cease to play.
But night rolls dark and still,
Oblivion's fabled river,
In whose sweet silence the restless will
Sleeps, and would sleep forever.

Shrill in the rustled maize
The boding cricket cries;

And through the East, where the dawn delays,
  Seaward the wild duck flies.
Noon comes with brazen glare,
  Stifling earth's song with splendor,
To drink the mists from the glittering air,
  And dew from the blossoms tender.

But when the night comes on,
  With cool and quiet sighs,
To shed fond thoughts on the soul alone,
  And rest in the tear-stained eyes, —
I lie beneath the stars,
  And life from their light is given,
Till my dreams escape from mortal wars,
  And sleep on the shore of heaven.

THE SUTTEE.

Come, thou dead image, to thy rest!
  The flashing embers wait for thee,
And heaped above my panting breast
  Lie faggots fit thy couch to be.

I know thee now, cold shape of clay,
  Whose life was but a thrill from mine!—
One gasp, and undeceiving day
  Showed the base thing no more divine.

Lo! I have framed a costly pyre;
  There lie those dreams with wandering eyes,
And hopes, too ashen now for fire,
  Strew pathways to the sacrifice.

I am a widow, and shall I
  Linger a living death away?
Here on the dead, I, too, will die,
  Quick! lest the flesh refuse to stay.

Burn! burn! glare upward to the skies,
  Paint the low hills and creeping night;
Louder the shrieking south-wind cries,
  And terror speeds the lessening light.

Slowly these eager tongues aspire;
  I shudder, though they set me free.
Go, coward senses, to the fire —
  But the wing'd soul, oh God! to Thee!

IMPLORA PACE.

WIND, that sighest over the snow,
  Mocking the sunshine cold and gay,
I reëcho thy voice of woe,
  Carry me on thy wings away!

Mist, that stretchest soft and far
  Over the mountains a purple haze,
Like thy shadow my sad thoughts are,
  Hide me safely from mortal gaze!

Waves, that lashing in ceaseless chime,
  Beat the earth till its rocks are sand,
Take on your tide this lingering time,
  Or bear its slave to a gentler strand.

Leaf, that hurriest madly by,
  Sport and spoil of the eager blast:
So from memory I would fly,
  So I cannot escape the past.

Blossoms, dead in your summer home,
  Sweet no longer, forgotten and lost,
Shall the withered heart to your silence come?
  Is there peace in the blight of frost?

NEW MOON.

Once, when the new moon glittered
  So slender in the West,
I looked across my shoulder,
  And a wild wish stirred my breast.

Over my white, right shoulder
  I looked at the silver horn,
And wished a wish at even
  To come to pass in the morn.

Whenever the new moon glittered,
  So slender and so fine,
I looked across my shoulder,
  And wished that wish of mine!

Now, when the West is rosy,
  And the snow-wreaths blush below,
And I see the light white crescent
  Float downward, soft and slow;

I never look over my shoulder,
  As I used to look before;
For my heart is older and colder,
  And now I wish no more!

DECEMBER XXXI.

There goes an old Gaffer over the hill,
  Thieving, and old, and gray;
He walks the green world, his wallet to fill,
  And carries good spoil away.

Into his bag he popped a king;
  After him went a friar,
Many a lady, with gay gold ring,
  Many a knight and squire.

He carried my true-love far away,
  He stole the dog at my door;
The wicked old Gaffer, thieving and gray,
  He'll never come by any more.

My little darling, white and fair,
  Sat in the door and spun;
He caught her fast by her silken hair,
  Before the child could run.

He stole the florins out of my purse,
  The sunshine out of mine eyes;
He stole my roses, and, what is worse,
  The gray old Gaffer told lies.

He promised fair when he came by,
  And laughed as he slipped away,
For every promise turned out a lie;
  But his tale is over to-day.

Good-by, old Gaffer! you'll come no more,
  You've done your worst for me.
The next gray robber will pass my door,
  There's nothing to steal or see!

LOTOS-LAND.

Oh, land beloved! oh, land unknown!
By what blue Rhine or rapid Rhone,
Or any river man hath known,
    Shall I arrive at thee?
Or by what mighty trackless seas,
Where the unwearied northern breeze
From dumb and frozen cavern flees
    Triumphant, to be free.

Or by what desert, red and vast,
Breathing the fevered tropic blast,
Shall my too lingering steps at last
    Attain to thy sweet shore?
Oh, plains serene! Oh, rivers rolled
Like babbling dreams o'er sands of gold!
Fair birds that do your pinions fold,
    And singing, cease to soar!

Skies, where such slumbrous mists are shed!
The heart forgets it ever bled,
And sleep lies on the lonely head,
    Forgetting and forgot.

There nothing has been or shall be,
But all things are eternally.
The tired soul may not think nor see
    Such quiet rules the spot;

For there is neither hope nor fear,
No hated thing and nothing dear,
Nor any troubled atmosphere,
    Nor anything but rest.
Such utter sleep, such thoughtlessness,
As might a mortal life redress
And set aside its deadly stress,
    From even a woman's breast.

Oh, land, dear land! sweet visioned shore,
That no man's footsteps may explore,
Nor any but a fool deplore,
    Yet would I slept in thee!
The jester tires of cap and bells,
The disenchanted laughs at spells,
The past all future lies foretells.
    Dear land, come true for me!

THE LAST REVOLUTION.

HURRAH! the mob is up again!
  I hear its distant rush and roar,
  Like mad seas surging on the shore;
But this sea shall not surge in vain.
Shout, bondsmen all, for freedom's reign —
      Hurrah!

A thousand, thousand hurrying feet,
  Resistless, heedless, trampling by:
  From the black East a shrieking cry;
The sound flies fast, the winds are fleet;
Hurrah! this liberty is sweet.
      Hurrah!

Hark! is't the roar of cannonades?
  A sullen thunder from afar —
  The grim, exulting psalm of war,
When deep in blood the victor wades:
No! 'tis the crashing barricades.
      Hurrah!

A shattered throne lies on the plain;
  Dead, at its foot, the hoary king.
  Shout for the gay republic — Spring!
Hurrah! it hath not come in vain,
This revolution of the rain.
          Hurrah!

IN THE HOSPITAL.

How the wind yells on the Gulf and prairie!
  How it rattles in the windows wide!
And the rats squeak like our old ship's rigging:
  I shall die with the turn of tide.

I've had a rough life on the ocean,
  And a tough life on the land;
Now I'm like a broken hulk in the dock-yard,—
  I can't stir foot nor hand.

There are green trees in the Salem graveyard;
  By the meeting-house steps they grow;
And there they put my poor old mother,
  The third in the leeward row.

There's the low red house on the corner,
  With a slant roof and a well-sweep behind,
And yellow-headed fennel in the garden,—
  How I see it when I go blind!

I wish I had a mug of cold water
  From the bottom of that old curb-well.
I wish my mother's face was here alongside,
  While I hear that tolling bell!

There's a good crop of corn in the meadow,
  And the biggest boy a'n't there to hoe;
They'll get in the apples and the pumpkins,
  But I've done my last chores below.

Don't you hear the Norther risin', doctor?
  How it yells and hollers, far and wide!
And the moon's a shinin' on that graveyard, —
  Hold on! I'm agoin' with the tide.

GRAY.

In the dead calm of night, when the stars are all shining,
The deep, silent shadows lie cold o'er my head,
And the wind, like a sad spirit, round the house pining,
Calls up from their quiet the tones of the dead.

Almost I can see them who rustle the curtain,
And flit past my cheek like a cold waft of air;
I hear their faint sighs and their footsteps uncertain,
I need not a vision to know they are there.

They call from the past all its bitterest warnings,
And trail the gray ghosts through my shuddering soul,
The nights of lone grief and the desolate mornings,
The long days of anguish that mocked my control.

Then comes the still angel who watches me ever,
And numbers the tears of my sleepless despair,

And their honey-sweet lips
  To no long kiss moving,
    Only die!

Oh, the love-red roses!
  With their golden centres,
Sweeter than spices;
  Where the south-wind enters,
And on the bee's track
  The butterfly ventures
    With his lie!

GRAY.

In the dead calm of night, when the stars are all shining,
The deep, silent shadows lie cold o'er my head,
And the wind, like a sad spirit, round the house pining,
Calls up from their quiet the tones of the dead.

Almost I can see them who rustle the curtain,
And flit past my cheek like a cold waft of air;
I hear their faint sighs and their footsteps uncertain,
I need not a vision to know they are there.

They call from the past all its bitterest warnings,
And trail the gray ghosts through my shuddering soul,
The nights of lone grief and the desolate mornings,
The long days of anguish that mocked my control.

Then comes the still angel who watches me ever,
And numbers the tears of my sleepless despair,

And for each sullen drop that assuages its fever,
  The angel stoops softly, and kisses my hair.

And at dawn I perceive in those shadowy tresses
  Bright silvery threads, as they fall o'er my breast,
And I know where the angel has left his caresses,
  A promise and pledge that he hastens my rest.

AT LAST.

THE old, old story o'er again —
Made up of passion, parting, pain.
He fought and fell, to live in fame,
But dying only breathed her name.

Some tears, most sad and innocent;
Some rebel thoughts, but all unmeant;
Then, with a silent, shrouded heart,
She turned to life and played her part.

Another man, who vowed and loved,
Her patient, pitying spirit moved,
Sweet hopes the dread of life beguiled, —
The lost love sighed, — the new love smiled.

So she was wed and children bore,
And then her widowed sables wore;
Her eyes grew dim, her tresses gray,
And dawned at length her dying day.

Her children gather, — some are gone,
Asleep beneath a lettered stone;
The living, cold with grief and fear,
Stoop down her whispering speech to hear.

No child she calls, no husband needs.
At death's sharp touch the old wound bleeds:
"Call him!" she cried, — her first love's name
Leapt from her heart with life's last flame.

MIDNIGHT.

The west-wind blows, the west-wind blew,
  The snow hissed cruelly,
All night I heard the baffled cry
  Of mariners on the sea.

I saw the icy shrouds and sail,
  The slippery, reeling deck,
And white-caps dancing pale with flame,
  The corpse-lights of the wreck.

The west-wind blows, the west-wind blew,
  And on its snowy way,
That hissed and hushed like rushing sand,
  My soul fled far away.

The snow went toward the morning hills
  In curling drifts of white,
But I went up to the gates of God
  Through all the howling night.

I went up to the gates of God.
  The angel waiting there,
Who keeps the blood-red keys of Heaven,
  Stooped down to hear my prayer.

"Dear keeper of the keys of Heaven,
  A thousand souls to-night
Are torn from life on land and sea,
  While life was yet delight.

"But I am tired of storms and pain;
  Sweet angel, let me in!
And send some strong heart back again,
  To suffer and to sin."

The angel answered — stern and slow —
  "How darest thou be dead,
While God seeks dust to make the street
  Where happier men may tread?

"Go back, and eat earth's bitter herbs,
  Go, hear its dead-bells toll;
Lie speechless underneath their feet,
  Who tread across thy soul.

"Go, learn the patience of the Lord
  Whose righteous judgments wait;

Thy murdered cry may cleave the ground,
But not unbar His gate."

Right backward, through the whirling snow —
Back, on the battling wind,
My soul crept slowly to its lair,
The body left behind.

The west-wind blows, the west-wind blew,
There are dead men on the sea,
And landsmen dead, in shrouding drifts —
But there is life in me.

"CHE SARA SARA."

SHE walked in the garden
  And a rose hung on a tree,
Red as heart's blood,
  Fair to see.
"Ah, kind south-wind,
  Bend it to me!"
But the wind laughed softly,
  And blew to the sea.

High on the branches,
  Far above her head,
Like a king's cup
  Round, and red.
"I am comely,"
  The maiden said,
"I have gold like shore-sand,
  I wish I were dead!

"Blushes and rubies
  Are not like a rose,

Through its deep heart
  Love-life flows.
Ah, what splendors
  Can give me repose!
What is all the world worth?
  I cannot reach my rose."

GONE.

A SILENT, odor-laden air,
  From heavy branches dropping balm;
A crowd of daisies milky fair,
  That sunward turn their faces calm.
So rapt, a bird alone may dare
  To stir their rapture with his psalm.

So falls the perfect day of June
  To moonlit eve, from dewy dawn,
With light winds rustling through the noon,
  And conscious roses half withdrawn,
In blushing buds that wake too soon,
  To flaunt their hearts on every lawn.

The wide content of summer's bloom,
  The peaceful glory of its prime;
Yet over all a brooding gloom,
  A desolation born of time;
As distant storm-caps tower and loom,
  And shroud the sun with heights sublime.

For they are vanished from the trees,
  And vanished from the thronging flowers,
Whose tender tones thrilled every breeze
  And sped with mirth the flying hours.
No form nor shape my sad eye sees ;
  No faithful spirit haunts these bowers.

Alone, alone, in sun or dew!
  One fled to heaven, of earth afraid ;
And one to earth, with eyes untrue
  And lips of faltering passion strayed.
Nor shall the strenuous years renew
  On any bough these leaves that fade.

Long summer-days shall come and go —
  No Summer brings the dead again.
I listen for that voice's flow
  And ache at heart with deepening pain.
And one fair face no more I know,
  Still living sweet, but sweet in vain.

CAIN.

HERE it found me — "Where is thy brother?"
  Out of the very heavens it fell,
Sharp as a peal of rattling thunder,
  Then the echo leapt up from hell.

He — Jehovah — "Where is thy brother?"
  I knew, He knew — the devil laughed.
He that gave me the staff to fell him.
  So the archer reviled the shaft!

Oh, my brother, my brother, my brother!
  Thy blood panted and throbbed in me.
We were children of one mother,
  Little children upon her knee.

Oh, my brother, my brother, my brother!
  Sad-eyed, tender, good, and true.
Never more on hill or valley,
  Never tracked through the morning dew.

I held up the staff before me.
  Down it crashed on the gentle head.
One live look of wondering sorrow,
  One sharp quiver — that was dead.

Thou! Thou gavest me a brother —
  Gave me a life to cast away —
Hast Thou in heaven such another?
  Hast Thou in heaven a sword to slay?

Hasten Thou — "Where is thy brother?"
  Voice my curst lips dare not name.
Hasten! write with thy fiery finger
  On my forehead the murderer's shame.

I am doomed — alone forever.
  Yet, so long as the slow years part,
Thou shalt brand new Cains with curses,
  Not on the forehead, but in the heart!

EBB AND FLOW.

'Tis something to have turned the tide
  That ebbed and ebbed and slid away,
Till all the sands lay bare and wide,
  A dreary level, bleak and gray.

The hidden rocks, the treacherous shore,
  Show black and steep above the sea;
The maddened breakers rave no more,
  Full fast the outward billows flee.

Rest for thy moment, turning tide!
  Then creep and ripple on the sand.
I fear no more thy waters wide,
  I know the dangers of the strand.

Now let thy white-caps foam and flow,
  The soul assured may laugh at fear,
And bear serene the heaviest woe,
  So that its utmost depths appear.

MAY.

THERE'S a bluebird sits on the apple-tree bough,
Singing merrily and gay.
Come, little blossoms, the Spring's here now,
And the sun shines warm all day.

Fast asleep in the leaves and grass,
Don't you hear the quick rain?
And the winds that whisper as they pass,
"The dear Spring's here again."

Push your soft leaves out of the ground,
Open your mist-blue eyes,
Hear the brook with its singing sound,
Look at the sunny skies.

All the drifts of the winter snow
Were frightened and fled away.
They left their place for the grass to grow,
And the merry moths to play.

Red buds shine on the maple-tree,
  The trailing May-blooms fair
Under their green leaves peep at me,
  For the Spring has kissed them there.

Come, little blossoms, you sleep too long!
  Purple and white and blue,
Open your buds to hear my song,
  The honey-bee waits for you.

NON SEQUITUR.

NEW, grassy scents, stir everywhere,
  And soft the southern winds complain:
Are these slow dews dropped out of air?
  And are they tears, or are they rain?

Some vague and sweet philosophy
  With flattering love-lips made reply, —
"Is not the omen good to thee?
  Both have their harvest by-and-by."

Then answered my indignant heart —
  "The rain is fresh, the rain is cold,
What wonder if the blossoms start
  When God bestows it on the mould!

"But hot and bitter tears of pain,
  The wild result of desperate hours,
What harvests black of blasted grain
  Should follow such unblessed showers?

"Go to, sweet voice! leave men to lie.
  The fond analogies you draw
Blazon their own futility, —
  Who judges man by nature's law?"

HERE.

SWEET summer-night, beside the sea,
Cast all thy sweet life over me!
Thy silence and serenity,
  Thy healing and content;
The rushing waves that fall and break
Unutterable music make,
And words that no man ever spake
  Are to its measure lent.

The salt wind kisses into rest
Both languid eye and fevered breast,
The cool gray rock, with sea-weeds drest,
  Gives shadow, still with strength;
The bitter and baptismal sea
With living water sprinkles me,
Slow patience sets her bondsman free,
  And blesses him at length.

There is a time in every tide
When surf and billow both subside,

And on the outward current glide
  Both shark and pirate sail;
The shipwrecked sailor, cast ashore,
Perceives afar that lessening roar,
And gives one desperate struggle more.
  Ah ! shall that struggle fail ?

MONOTROPA.

September 5, 1857.

Loves serene, uncarnate Graces!
Born of pure dreams in lonely places,
Where the black untrodden earth
Rejects the dancing sunshine's mirth,
And slow leaves, dropping through the wood,
Stir to sound the solitude.
Through what tranquil, odorous airs,
Undisturbed by sighs or prayers,
Paler than pale alabaster
Wrought to life by some old master,
Did ye into vision rise,
And nocturnal moths surprise?

Clustered in undraperied whiteness,
Pierced by stars to lucent brightness,
Cooler than a baby's lips,
Pure as dew that nightly drips,

Utterly intact and calm,
Cold to summer's rapturous balm,
So divine that in ye lingers
A shuddering dread of mortal fingers,
Though their tips be pink and fine,
Under the caress ye pine,
Blackened with the passion-fever
That your cool bells shun forever.

Sweetest souls of beauty-lovers,
Above your cups the gold bee hovers,
In sequestered maze and awe,
Repelled by instinct's sacred law;
Knowing well no sweetness lies
In your frosted chalices.
Never bird, nor bee, nor moth,
Inebriate with sunny sloth,
Dare intrude on hallowed ground,
Cease thyself, vain rhythmic sound!

EXOGENESIS.

THE curving beach and shining bay,
Stretch from the cliff-foot far away,
Where sailing dreams of ships go by
And trace their spars against the sky.
A belt of woodland, dense and dark,
The distant beacon's flashing spark,
The moth-white sails that wing-and-wing
Up from the purple ocean spring;—
One and all, in the perfect hour,
Open to life its perfect flower;
Though the ardent rose is dim and dead,
Though the cool Spring-daisies all are fled,
The lily unfolds its tintless calm
And the golden anthers are spiced with balm.

Come, my soul, from thy silent cell!
Know the healing of Nature's spell.
The soft wild waves that rush and leap,
Sing one song from the hoary deep;

The south-wind knows its own refrain
As it speeds the cloud o'er heaven's blue main.
"Lose thyself, thyself to win:
Grow from without thee, not within."

Leave thy thought and care alone,
Let the dead for the dead make moan;
Gather from earth and air and sea
The pulseless peace they keep for thee.
Ring on ring of sight and sound
Shall hide thy heart in a calm profound, —
Where the works of men and the ways of earth
Shall never enter with tears or mirth,
And the love of kind shall kinder be
From nature than humanity.

CAPTIVE.

THE Summer comes, the Summer dies,
  Red leaves whirl idly from the tree,
But no more cleaving of the skies,
  No southward sunshine waits for me!

You shut me in a gilded cage,
  You deck the bars with tropic flowers,
Nor know that freedom's living rage
  Defies you through the listless hours.

What passion fierce, what service true,
  Could ever such a wrong requite?
What gift, or clasp, or kiss from you
  Were worth an hour of soaring flight?

I beat my wings against the wire,
  I pant my trammelled heart away;
The fever of one mad desire
  Burns and consumes me all the day.

What care I for your tedious love,
  For tender word or fond caress?
I die for one free flight above,
  One rapture of the wilderness!

DOUBT.

THE bee knows honey,
  And the blossoms light,
Day the dawning,
  Stars the night;
The slow, glad river
  Knows its sea;
Is it true, Love,
  I know not thee?

When the Summer
  Brings snow-drifts piled,
When the planets
  Go wandering wild,
When the old hill-tops
  Valleys be,—
Tell me true, Love,
  Shall I know thee?

Where'er I wander,
  By sea or shore,

A dim, sweet vision
  Flies fast before,
Its lingering shadow
  Floats over me; —
I know thy shade, Love,
  Do I know thee?

"Rest in thy dreaming,
  Child divine!
What grape-bloom knoweth
  Its fiery wine?
Only the sleeper
  No sun can see;
He that doubteth
  Knows not me."

SAMSON AGONISTES.

December 2, 1859.

YOU bound and made your sport of him, Philistia!
You set your sons at him to flout and jeer;
You loaded down his limbs with heavy fetters;
Your mildest mercy was a smiling sneer.

One man amidst a thousand who defied him —
One man from whom his awful strength had fled, —
You brought him out to lash him with your vengeance,
Ten thousand curses on one hoary head!

You think his eyes are closed and blind forever,
Because you seared them to this mortal day;
You draw a longer breath of exultation,
Because your conqueror's power has passed away.

Oh, fools! his arms are round your temple-pillars;
Oh, blind! his strength divine begins to wake;—
Hark! the great roof-tree trembles from its centre,
Hark! how the rafters bend and swerve and shake!

"THE HARVEST IS PAST."

Go, dead Summer, o'er the seas away;
Autumn at her vespers now will kneel and pray,
Sunlit vapors on the mountains stray,
Red grows the round moon, — Summer goes away.

Go, dead Summer! the birds will care,
They will follow on the soft sea-air,
While the south-wind breathes a low prayer,
And the perfumed pine-leaves thy shroud prepare.

Go, dead Summer! go, to come again.
All things rise but madness and pain.
New green grasses flicker on the plain,
Only a lost life comes not again.

One dead Summer never shall return.
In its ashes no red embers burn.
Over it vainly the tired soul may yearn.
It is dead, wept, buried: how can it return?

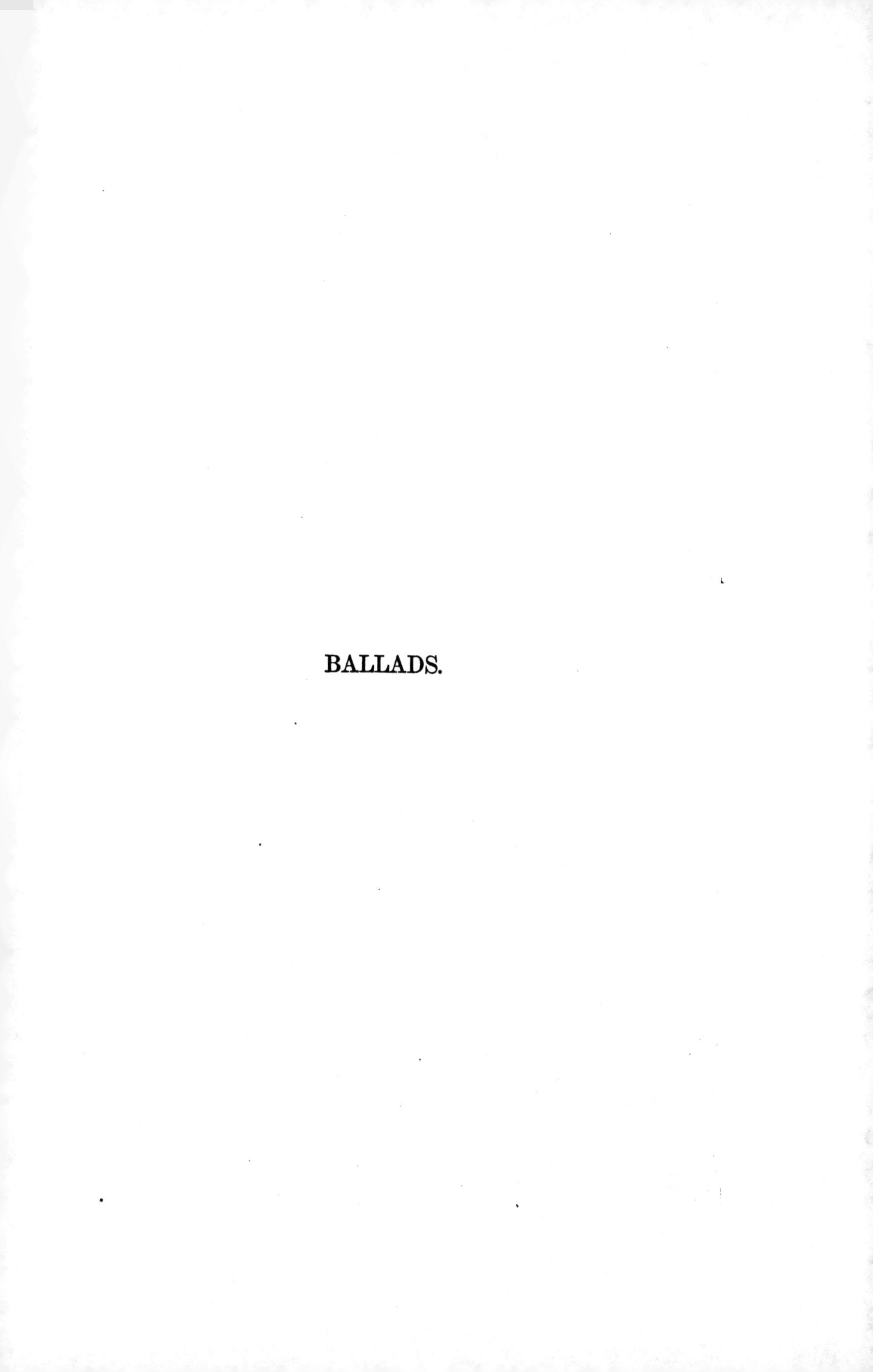

BALLADS.

BALLADS.

ROSALIND.

HIGH on the hills Lord Heron he dwells,
  Rosalind sings on the moors below,
Faint as the sea in its singing shells,
  Up to the castle her soft notes go.

Young Lord Heron has left his state,
  Donned a doublet of hodden-gray;
Stolen out at the postern-gate,
  A silly shepherd, to wander away.

Rosalind keeps the heart of a child,
  Tender and gentle and true is she;
Colin the shepherd is comely and mild,
  Tending his flocks by valley and lea.

Never shepherd has whispered before
  Words she hears at the close of day: —

"Rose of roses, I love thee more —
  More than the tenderest words can say.

"Though I seem but a shepherd lad,
  Down from a stately race I came;
In silks and jewels I'll have thee clad,
  And Lady of Heron shall be thy name."

Rosalind blushed a rosy red,
  Turned as pale as the hawthorn's blow,
Folded her kirtle over her head,
  And sped away like a startled doe.

"Rose of roses, come back to me!
  Leave me never!" Lord Heron cried, —
"Never!" echoed from hill and lea,
  "Never!" the lonely cliffs replied.

Loud he mourned a year and a day,
  But Lady Alice was fair to see;
The bright sun blesses his bridal day,
  And the castle-bells ring merrily.

Over the moors, like a rolling knell,
  Rosalind hears them slowly peal;
Low she mourned — "I loved him well, —
  Better I loved his mortal weal.

"Rest, Lord Heron, in Alice's arms,
  She is a lady of high degree;
Rosalind had but a peasant's charms,
  Ye had rued the day ye wedded me!"

Lord Heron he dwells in the castle high,
  Rosalind sleeps on the moors below.
He loved, to live; and she loved, to die;
  Which loved truest, the angels know!

FREMONT'S RIDE

NIGHT on creek and rancho, bound in sleep we lay,
Dreaming of señoritas and maidens far away,
The heavy tropic moonlight its plates of silver spread
Over Sonoma's valleys, and the gully's rocky bed.

Through the dreams, like thunder, came, rolling loud
and long
At the gate of ranch and corral, the beat of knuckles
strong:
"Boys! rouse up! they're on us. Quick! the gate-
way bends.
Who's out there?" "Americans! Open the gate
to friends."

Through the portal pouring, eager, hot, and grim,
A hundred bearded horsemen stream in the mid-
night dim.
First and least and greatest, set on a mustang stout,
The leader of the hundred, the chief of hunt and
scout.

Keen as sword or bullet came his rapid speech:
"Give me your horses, Señor! the Puebla I must reach!
The States shall pay you eagles. Quick! for I must be gone,
I'm bound to see Los Angelos before six days are done!"

"But, Señor!" — "Quick, the horses! Los Angelos is far,
Six hundred miles of mud and flood, — the States have gone to war.
I must be in at the death-fight! Oh, I shall make good speed!"
Away went the pale vaqueros — away went every steed.

Gallop, gallop, gallop! over stock and stone,
Through the rocky gully, through creeks of the wild cañon,
Over plain and valley, past the lonely ranch,
Grazing clumps of chapparal, swimming the flooded branch.

Dead dropped mare and mustang. "Off with saddle and bit, —
Mount another, and forward! the fight is raging yet!"

Through San Pablo tearing — tearing through Monterey —
Over bluffs and prairies gallop the mad array.

The sixth day in the morning they reach a river wide;
The bravest pause before it — Fremont is in the tide!
Over, over, over! follow him to the death!
The swollen waves roll deeper, and two are swept beneath.

Horse and rider struggle — "Forward! the brink is won!
Ride, ride for the Puebla! ride lest the fight be done!"
"Hurrah! Fremont and Freedom! Los Angelos we sight;
Now for the Mexican devils! now for a bloody fight!"

So the sharp tornado whirls from a swooping cloud, —
So comes the sudden lightning down from its lurid shroud:
One rattling shout of thunder, then to the thickest fight —
The dying plunge and quiver, the living take to flight.

They shout from the Presidio, they shout across the
plain,
And the great heart of his country sends back the
shout again.
Hurrah, for the Prairie Hunter! Hurrah for the
People's Pride!
Hurrah! Fremont and Freedom! Hurrah for the
hundred's ride!

BASILE RENAUD.

THE summer sun bedecks Anjou,
The harvest time keeps promise true,
And I have kept my faith with you
    Basile Renaud!
The sun forsakes my dungeon walls,
Across the fosse no shadow falls,
I hear no answer to my calls,
    Basile Renaud!

My name was Clara Madaillon.
I had a sister, I had one
Who should have been a hooded nun,
    That made us three:
Marie and I dwelt in the tower,
But Angelique forsook her dower,
And in a convent made her bower,
    The convent of St. Brie.

There came a lover to our lands,
I wove my hair in shining bands

And put bright jewels on my hands,
  Basile Renaud!
You looked at me as at a star,
You said I was as cold and far;
I laugh now, thinking what you are,
  Basile Renaud!

He gave me a betrothal ring,
I learned for him to smile and sing;
"Proud Clara, have you found your king?"
  They said to me.
So from the nuns came Angelique
For her farewells; oh! she was meek,
With yellow tresses down her cheek,
  And blue eyes soft to see!

My love beheld her tender face,
Her little hands and gentle grace, —
How dared you give her my right place,
  Basile Renaud?
I scoffed at her, I hated him;
And Marie said — "His eyes are dim;
Were't me — " So ran thy requiem,
  Basile Renaud!

We took our counsel, nor would show
More signs of vengeance than the snow

That hides a traveller far below
 Its shining drift.
The winter nights came on too fast,
But they two did not hear the blast
That howled, and howled, and shivered past,
 And muttered in the rift.

One night we were both grave and gay,
For Angelique had gone away,
And one was sad, but two would play,
 Basile Renaud.
The firelight flickered in the hall,
The sconces burned with torches tall;
I, blinded, hunted to the wall
 Basile Renaud.

"Will you be hunter?" Marie said;
She tied the kerchief round his head;
I had a knife — and it grew red —
 But not with flame.
His brow bent down upon my arm.
I laughed to see the working charm.
He had no will to do us harm,
 Nor breath to murmur blame.

They haled us to a prison high,
Where all day long thick shadows lie,

And in broad daylight we shall die,
    Basile Renaud!
But I had vengeance! though there be
Only one sister left of three —
Angelique in the nunnery —
    Basile Renaud!

THE DEATH OF TANKERFIELD.

The death of holy Tankerfield,
  That martyr of the Lord's,
And his great worth I do set forth
  As seasonable words.

In young King Edward's blessed time,
  A Papist vile was he;
Uncleansèd from the filthy slime
  Of vain idolatry.

But when it pleased the Lord most high
  To take the king away,
Unto his everlasting rest,
  To be with him alway, —

When bloody Mary's reign began,
  Wherein the flock of Christ
Did wander through the valleys low,
  And stumble in the mist, —

Then, as he saw what cruel pains
  From men they did endure,
And suffered pangs of many deaths
  To make their glory sure —

His heart was moved and stirred within
  To see their evil tide,
And that foul church which wrought the sin
  He might no more abide.

But turned unto the sacred Word,
  To light his darksome soul;
And learned to leave that faith abhorred
  That would his mind control.

And did his feeble voice uplift
  To make a protest bold, —
Renouncing all the devil's works,
  To which he clave of old.

Thereat unto his house there came
  A man of cruel mind,
By name one Byrd, who thought no shame
  This godly youth to bind.

Before the judge they haled him then,
  Who sent him back apace,

Unto a doleful prison-cell,
  Where he remained a space.

But when before the court he came,
  To answer for his faith,
Of Christ the Lord he was not shamed,
  But owned him unto death.

So, when the summer-tide was come,
  And all the fields were green,
And flowers upon the dewy meads
  Were joyful to be seen,

They brought him from his dungeon-cell
  Unto a certain Inn,
And bade him to remember well
  The wages of his sin.

For that he never more should see
  The rising of the sun.
"Then," with a cheerful voice, quoth he,
  "Good Lord, thy will be done!

"Now, bring me here a cup of wine,
  Withal a wheaten cake,
To keep the Supper of the Lord,
  Ere I my end do make.

"I may not have a minister
 To break this bread to me,
But by thy passion, gracious Lord,
 Lay not the sin to me!

"I fain would keep thy feast again
 Before I drink it new,
To aid my flesh in deathly pain,
 And keep my spirit true."

So, giving thanks, he took the bread,
 And drank the sacred wine,
Which now in heaven he doth partake
 From chalices divine.

Then prayed he them to light a fire,
 That he his strength might try;
The host did grant him his desire,
 And stood amazèd by:

For, lo! he stretched his naked foot
 Into the scorching flame,
But bone and sinew quivering shrank,
 And loud he spake in pain:—

"Ho, flesh! thou wilt not gladly burn,
 But spirit shall endure;

Ho, sense! thou wouldst from glory turn,
  But soul thou shalt make sure!"

Then, as the time drew on apace
  That he by fire should die,
He kneeled again and prayed for grace
  To bear his agony.

Then, with a calm and pleasant smile,
  Saith he, — "However long
The day may seem, yet at the last
  It rings for even-song."

The sheriffs brought him to a green,
  Hard by the abbey-wall,
And seeing there the fagots piled,
  They spake aloud to all.

"A dinner sharp is mine to-day,"
  Quoth he, with joyful faith,
"But I shall sup on heavenly cates,
  And triumph over death."

When he was fettered to the stake,
  They heaped the pile full high,
And called a priest, with subtle words
  To shake his constancy.

But loudly he denied the mass
  And all the works of Rome,
So might not Babylonish tricks
  Delay his passage home.

A certain knight, who stood thereby,
  Laid hold upon his hand.
Quoth he, "Good brother in the Lord,
  Be strong in Christ, and stand."

"Oh, sir!" the martyr made reply,
  "I give you thanks indeed.
May God be lauded, I am strong!"
  With that they bade him heed.

And set the fire unto the pile:
  When, as the flame shot high,
Unto the strong and mighty One
  He powerfully did cry.

Yea, from the depths uplifted he
  A cry for help to God,
And homeward then, on fiery wings,
  Right joyfully he rode.

WHITE AND RED.

ROSES and daisies, lovingly they grow,
Redder than a sunset, milkier than snow;
Side by side they glitter in the grasses lithe,
Side by side they wither, swept before the scythe.

Down in the valley sits Lina at her wheel,
While along the mountains twilight-shadows steal,
Singing through the daylight softly as a bird,
All that summer whispers in her song you heard.

Night came on like morning, cold and still and gray,
Over Alpine summits a threat of tempest lay,
Lina stopped her singing, and trimmed her taper bright,
Her lover on the mountains watched for the beacon-light.

All night long she waited, listening to the rain,
That muttered in the fir-trees and rustled on the pane.

Shrieking like a spirit, the morning west-wind blew,
And flickered in the casement the watch-light burning true.

Lina to the threshold turned her trembling feet.
Saints in heaven, preserve her, such a sight to meet!
The dead-white face before her, — the roaring stream below.
The water-sprite, at dead of night, had wrought her mortal woe.

Two biers to the chapel bear the friars gray,
Over two pale corpses the funeral mass they say.
Lina and her lover are gathered to their rest, —
So we one day shall pass away, and live among the blest.

Roses and daisies! — through the world they shine,
Blood-red blooms of sorrow, dreams of peace divine,
Only up in glory the quiet angels wear
Wreaths of spotless calmness, lilies pure and fair.

FRONTIER BALLADS.

I.

AFTER THE CAMANCHES.

SADDLE, saddle, saddle!
  Mount and gallop away!
Over the dim green prairie,
  Straight on the track of day.
Spare not spur for mercy,
  Hurry with shout and thong,
Fiery and tough is the mustang,
  The prairie is wide and long.

Saddle, saddle, saddle!
  Leap from the broken door
Where the brute Camanche entered
  And the white-foot treads no more.
The hut is burned to ashes,
  There are dead men stark outside,
But only a long dark ringlet
  Left of the stolen bride.

Go, like the east-wind's howling!
  Ride with death behind.
Stay not for food or slumber,
  Till the thieving wolves ye find!
They came before the wedding,
  Swifter than prayer or priest;
The bridemen danced to bullets,
  The wild dogs ate the feast.

Look to rifle and powder!
  Fasten the knife-belt sure;
Loose the coil of the lasso,
  Make the loop secure;
Fold the flask in the poncho,
  Fill the pouch with maize,
And ride as if to-morrow
  Were the last of living days!

Saddle, saddle, saddle!
  Redden spur and thong;
Ride like the mad tornado,
  The track is lonely and long.
Spare not horse nor rider;
  Fly for the stolen bride;
Bring her home on the crupper,
  A scalp on either side!

LOST ON THE PRAIRIE.

Oh, my baby, my child, my darling!
  Lost and gone in the prairie wild;
Mad gray wolves from the forest snarling,
  Snarling for thee, my little child!

Lost, lost! gone forever!
  Gay snakes rattled and charmed and sung;
On thy head the sun's fierce fever,
  Dews of death on thy white lip hung!

Dead and pale in the moonlight's glory,
  Cold and dead by the black oak-tree;
Only a small shoe, stained and gory,
  Blood-red, tattered, — comes home to me.

Over the grass that rolls, like ocean,
  On and on to the blue, bent sky,
Something comes with a hurried motion,
  Something calls with a choking cry, —

"Here, here! not dead, but living!"
  God! Thy goodness — what can I pray?
Blessed more in this second giving,
  Laid in happier arms to-day.

Oh, my baby, my child, my darling!
  Wolf and snake and the lonely tree
Still are rustling, hissing, snarling;
  Here's my baby come back to me!

III.

DONE FOR.

A WEEK ago to-day, when red-haired Sally
  Down to the sugar-camp came to see me,
I saw her checked frock coming down the valley,
  Far as anybody's eyes could see.
Now I sit before the camp-fire,
  And I can't see the pine-knots blaze,
Nor Sally's pretty face a-shining,
  Though I hear the good words she says.

A week ago to-night I was tired and lonely,
  Sally was gone back to Mason's fort,
And the boys by the sugar-kettles left me only;
  They were hunting coons for sport.
By there snaked a painted Pawnee,
  I was asleep before the fire;
He creased my two eyes with his hatchet,
  And scalped me to his heart's desire.

There they found me on the dry tussocks lying,
  Bloody and cold as a live man could be;

A hoot-owl on the branches overhead was crying,
  Crying murder to the red Pawnee.
They brought me to the camp-fire,
  They washed me in the sweet white spring;
But my eyes were full of flashes,
  And all night my ears would sing.

I thought I was a hunter on the prairie,
  But they saved me for an old blind dog;
When the hunting-grounds are cool and airy,
  I shall lie here like a helpless log.
I can't ride the little wiry pony,
  That scrambles over hills high and low;
I can't set my traps for the cony,
  Or bring down the black buffalo.

I'm no better than a rusty, bursted rifle,
  And I don't see signs of any other trail;
Here by the camp-fire blaze I lie and stifle,
  And hear Jim fill the kettles with his pail.
It's no use groaning. I like Sally,
  But a Digger squaw wouldn't have me!
I wish they hadn't found me in the valley, —
  It's twice dead not to see!

IV.

BEE-HUNTING.

WHEN the sky is red and hazy,
And the winds are warm and lazy,
And the blackbirds chatter crazy,
  Hurrah for the forest free!
The Summer days are over,
The bees have sucked the clover,
And the honey-birds call and hover
  Over the hollow tree.

Catch the bee where you find him,
Follow on straight behind him,
Till home to his nest you've lined him,
  Then sing for the match and axe.
Gather bark from the birches,
Moss where the screech-owl perches,
And when the fire smokes and smirches,
  Chop till the tree-trunk cracks.

Ho, boys! stand from under!
Hear it topple and thunder;

Then rush in for the plunder ;
  Dripping from comb and chip;
Clear as sunlight shining,
It drops from the waxen lining,
Sugar that needs no fining,
  Fit for a woman's lip.

Heap it in pail and kettle,
Never go off with a little,
Quick! or the bees will settle
  On something beside the trees.
Off with the stolen treasure!
The bears may take their pleasure,
Where we have left good measure
  For them and the drowsy bees.

When the sky is red and hazy,
And the winds are warm and lazy,
And the blackbirds chatter crazy,
  Hurrah for the forest free!
The Summer days are over,
But we get the best of the clover,
Where the honey-birds call and hover:
  Out of a hollow tree:

TRANSLATIONS.

TRANSLATIONS.

THE MOURNING DOVE.

(From the Hebrew.)

ALAS! for I am flying
  Through deserts lone and dreary,
In rocks and caverns lying,
  With downcast soul and weary;
The tempest whirling o'er me,
  My fluttering wing repelling,
The forest spread before me,
  One lonely bough my dwelling.

My God forsakes the altar
  Whereon His anger burneth,
And where my weak steps falter,
  His wrath a whirlwind turneth;
I pined for strange caresses, —
  For aliens madly yearning
Betrayed the hand that blesses,
  And foes beheld my turning.

But since His love departed,
  Mine eyes have failed with weeping,
My life is broken-hearted,
  Its light in darkness sleeping.
Better the grave's dominion
  Than thus forsaken flying,
And blessed death's shadowy pinion
  To souls in anguish crying.

Behold the bird-mates greeting
  With fond and tender kisses,
Where hearts caress, and, meeting,
  Find Eden's purest blisses;
Their rest is fixed forever,
  Deep in the green boughs lying,
Where olive-branches quiver,
  And lilies sweet are sighing.

But I am lost and weary,
  No home for me remaining;
Among the cleft rocks dreary,
  With briers and thorns complaining.
My God forsakes the altar
  Whereon His anger burneth;
And where my weak steps falter,
  His wrath a whirlwind turneth.

Fierce eagles, sunward turning,
  Scream to their mates at even;
But to the lone dove mourning,
  Nor mate, nor home is given.
Earth with their rapine groaneth,
  They rest in peace unheeding;
But when the just man moaneth,
  The heavens refuse his pleading!

Return, my God! my glory!
  Thou, oh, my consolation!
Hear Thou the fearful story,
  And rise for my salvation.
Unveil Thy love's clear shining,
  Above mine anguish hover,
And when I lie repining,
  My sins with mercy cover!

Thus in the night I hearkened
  Grief like a hushed sea swelling;
Jehovah's fear hath darkened
  On every human dwelling.
I know when man assaileth
  The ear of heaven with moaning,
That mortal courage faileth,
  My people's heart is groaning!

POUR ELISE FRISELL.

(Chateaubriand.)

THE coffin sinks, and sink the roses white,
  A father's tribute in his sorrowing hour:
Earth, that bore both, now hiding from the light,
  Young girl, young flower!

Ah, ne'er return them to this world profane!
  This world where mourning, anguish, sorrow, lower.
Winds bruise and scatter, sunbeams burn and stain,
  Young girl, young flower!

Though sleep'st, poor child, unbowed by years of care,
  Fearing the task and heat of day no more;
Both just outlived their morning fresh and fair,
  Young girl, young flower!

Thy father bends above thy last repose,
  Pale are the lines that mark his temples hoar;
Around thy root, old oak, Time ruthless mows,
  Young girl, — young flower!

LA FLEUR ET LE PAPILLON.

(Victor Hugo.)

A FLOWER said to the butterfly of heaven,
Depart no more!
Ah! see what diverse fates to us are given,—
I stand, you soar!

Yet we both love, and far from mortals dwelling
Pass the bright hours:
Like in ourselves, and as they still are telling,
We both are flowers.

Alas! earth chains me, thou in air art flying,—
Stern destiny!
I would embalm thy flight with odorous sighing,
Breathed through the sky.

But no! thou wanderest far, 'mid countless flowers,
On pinions fleet:
I watch my shadow through the weary hours
Turn at my feet.

Thou fliest, then returnest, still adorning
Thy various spheres;
Still finding me with every new-born morning
Bathed in my tears.

Oh! that our love may still be true and tender,
My king divine!
Take root as I, or give me wings of splendor
Like unto thine!

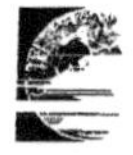

LE JUIF ERRANT.

(Béranger.)

Christian, to a suffering traveller
  Give a draught of water at thy gate!
I am he, the ever-wand'ring Hebrew,
  Hurried on by whirlwinds to my fate.
Never older, though surviving ages,
  Toward the world's far end I turn mine eyes,
Every night I hope will know no morrow,
  Every morning sees the sun arise.
      Evermore
  Turns the earth I wander o'er;
      Evermore, evermore!

Ah! for eighteen lingering cycles,
  Over silent Greek and Roman ashes,
Over ruins of a thousand kingdoms,
  Me the wild, unsparing whirlwind dashes.
I have seen the germ of virtue fruitless,—

I have seen how fruitful ill can be,
And to live beyond the old world's glory,
Two new worlds arising from the sea.
Evermore
Turns the earth I wander o'er;
Evermore, evermore!

God for punishment hath changed me.
Love to all that die my worn heart bears.
But the wretch for whom a home is smiling,
Far from all the sudden whirlwind tears.
Many a beggar comes with eye imploring
For the boon wherewith alone I bless,
Who can find no pause to grasp, in passing,
Even the hand I long in his to press.
Evermore
Turns the earth I wander o'er;
Evermore, evermore!

Underneath the tree in blossom,
On the turf, or where cool waves rejoice,
If I strive to soothe my lonely anguish,
Loud I hear the whirlwind's raging voice.
Ah! what matters it, thou angry heaven,
This short respite snatched from wrath divine?
Is then all eternity sufficient
To repose from such a toil as mine?

Evermore
Turns the earth I wander o'er;
Evermore, evermore!

Sometimes bright and happy children,
Of my own, retrace the imaged forms;
If the sight refresh my longing vision,
Lo! the whirlwind hurls its furious storms.
Ah! old men, what price untold could tempt ye
Me to envy life's unsetting day?
These fair children whom I smile in greeting—
Soon my feet shall brush their dust away.
Evermore
Turns the earth I wander o'er;
Evermore, evermore!

If the city of my fathers
Not entirely to the dust has gone,
And I strive to linger by its ruins,
Still the fearful whirlwind thunders "On!"
"On!" and also cries that voice of terror,
"Rest remains when all beside shall die.
Do not they who sleep among thy fathers
In their tomb, thy place of rest deny?"
Evermore
Turns the earth I wander o'er;
Evermore, evermore!

I outraged, with laugh inhuman,
  Thine expiring pangs, thou Son of God!
Look! beneath my feet the road is flying —
  Hark! the whirlwind hurries me abroad. —
Ye whose hearts to charity are strangers,
  Tremble at the awful doom I bear.
'Tis not God's divine, eternal nature,
  'Tis humanity avenged here!
        Evermore
      Turns the earth I wander o'er;
        Evermore, evermore!

MAUDIT PRINTEMPS.

(Béranger.)

I SAW her through my window-pane
  All Winter smiling at her own ;
Unknown I loved, was loved again,
  And kisses crossed that both had thrown.
Through the old lime-trees' branches gray,
  Our sole delight, fond looks to turn;
But now between us leaves will play.
  Why, hateful Spring, wilt thou return?

Ah! I shall lose her in their shade,
  The lovely angel over there!
Who fed with crumbs, — dear, tender maid! —
  Poor birds that felt the frosty air.
She calls them, and the cares she shows
  To lovers' silent signals turn.
Ah! what so fair as Winter's snows!
  Why, hateful Spring, must thou return?

Depart, and I should see her now,
  Rising, when sleep has passed away,
Fresh as they paint Aurora's brow,
  Parting the curtains of the day.
And still my lips would breathe at night,
  "Alas! my star has ceased to burn!
She sleeps — no more I see her light."—
  Why, hateful Spring, must thou return?

I pine till Winter comes again.
  Would that I heard, with welcome sound,
Tinkling against the window-pane,
  The hailstones rattle and rebound.
If all thine ancient realm were mine,
  Thy gales, thy flowers, thy warmth I'd spurn,
Since here no more her smiles can shine.
  Why, hateful Spring, must thou return.

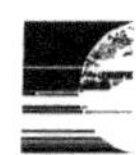

LA SYLPHIDE.

(Béranger.)

E'EN reason is not always wise,
  Her torch-light is not always clear,
For your existence she denies,
  Sylphs! charming people of the air!
Thrusting her ægis dull aside,
  That rested on my curious eyes,
Lately I saw a sylphide glide.
  Gay sylphs, be my divinities!

Your cradles are the roses' breasts,
  Of Zephyr and Aurora born;
And in your brilliant changes rests
  The secret light of pleasure's morn.
Our tears ye dry with gentle breath,
  Ye keep unstained the azure skies,
My sylphide's charms demand my faith,
  Gay sylphs, be my divinities!

Ah! well I knew her dwelling-place,
  When, at the ball, or at the feast,

I saw her childish form of grace
  Most lovely when arrayed the least,
A ribbon lost, — a jewel gone, —
  More fair as each adornment flies,
Of all your race the loveliest one.
  Gay sylphs, be my divinities!

She adds a thousand graces new
  To your caprices sweet and wild;
A child that's spoiled, perhaps 'tis true,
  But ah! 'tis sylphs have spoiled the child.
I see beneath that listless air
  What dreaming love dwells in her eyes;
Ye who make tender hearts your care,
  Gay sylphs, be my divinities!

But in her gentle childhood dwells
  A mind arrayed in fairer light
Than e'er your dream-enchanting spells
  Threw o'er the sleep of young delight.
From sparkling wit aloft she springs
  And bears me with her to the skies;
Ye who possessed her borrowed wings,
  Gay sylphs, be my divinities!

Ah! like a meteor's rapid train,
  Too quickly to our eyes denied, —

Shall I behold her form again?
  Perhaps some sylph has called her bride.
No! like the bees' mysterious queen,
  In some strange land her empire lies;
Conduct me to that realm serene,
  Gay sylphs, be my divinities!

LA MOUCHE.

(Béranger.)

Amid our frolic laughter's sound,
'Mid tinkling cups and music gay,
What murmuring insect hovers round
Returning when 'tis chased away?
Some Power, I think, who hovers near,
Jealous of bliss it can't annoy;
Permit it not to murmur here,
To murmur at our joy!

Transformed into a hideous fly,
My friends, it is — I know the guest —
Reason, that scolding deity,
Enraged at such a joyous feast!
The thunder sounds, the storm draws near,
Her dark frown threatens to destroy;
Permit her not to murmur here,
To murmur at our joy!

'Tis Reason, whispering low to me;
"Thy years should calmer pleasures bring;

Cease drinking, laughter, jollity,
  No longer love, no longer sing!"
Her belfry rings its peal of fear
  At every flame of sweet alloy;
Permit her not to murmur here,
  To murmur at our joy!

'Tis Reason! ah! beware, Lisette!
  On thee she longs her sting to prove:
Ye powers! in that fair neck 'tis set —
  The red blood springs, haste every Love!
Pursue the wretch's flight of fear,
  And with your blows her life destroy;
Permit her not to murmur here,
  To murmur at our joy!

Triumph! I see her drowning gasp
  Deep in the cup Lisette hath poured, —
Triumph! to Pleasure's rightful grasp
  Now let the sceptre be restored!
A zephyr shakes her crown with fear,
  A fly can all our peace destroy, —
But fear no more its murmurs here,
  Its murmurs at our joy!

THE END.

☞ Any Books in this list will be sent free of postage, on receipt of price.

BOSTON, 135 WASHINGTON STREET,
DECEMBER, 1860.

A LIST OF BOOKS

PUBLISHED BY

TICKNOR AND FIELDS.

Sir Walter Scott.

ILLUSTRATED HOUSEHOLD EDITION OF THE WAVERLEY NOVELS. 50 volumes. In portable size, 16mo. form. Now Complete. Price 75 cents a volume.

The paper is of fine quality; the stereotype plates are not old ones repaired, the type having been cast expressly for this edition. The Novels are illustrated with capital steel plates engraved in the best manner, after drawings and paintings by the most eminent artists, among whom are Birket Foster, Darley, Billings, Landseer, Harvey, and Faed. This Edition contains all the latest notes and corrections of the author, a Glossary and Index; and some curious additions, especially in "Guy Mannering" and the "Bride of Lammermoor;" being the fullest edition of the Novels ever published. *The notes are at the foot of the page*,—a great convenience to the reader.

Any of the following Novels sold separate.

WAVERLEY, 2 vols.
GUY MANNERING, 2 vols.
THE ANTIQUARY, 2 vols.
ROB ROY, 2 vols.
OLD MORTALITY, 2 vols.
BLACK DWARF, LEGEND OF MONTROSE, } 2 vols.
HEART OF MID LOTHIAN, 2 vols.
BRIDE OF LAMMERMOOR, 2 vols.
IVANHOE, 2 vols.
THE MONASTERY, 2 vols.
THE ABBOT, 2 vols.
KENILWORTH, 2 vols.
THE PIRATE, 2 vols.
THE FORTUNES OF NIGEL, 2 vols.
PEVERIL OF THE PEAK, 2 vols.
QUENTIN DURWARD, 2 vols.
ST. RONAN'S WELL, 2 vols.
REDGAUNTLET, 2 vols.
THE BETROTHED, THE HIGHLAND WIDOW, } 2 vols.
THE TALISMAN, TWO DROVERS, MY AUNT MARGARET'S MIRROR, THE TAPESTRIED CHAMBER, THE LAIRD'S JOCK. } 2 vols.
WOODSTOCK, 2 vols.
THE FAIR MAID OF PERTH, 2 vols.
ANNE OF GEIERSTEIN, 2 vols.
COUNT ROBERT OF PARIS, 2 vols.
THE SURGEON'S DAUGHTER, CASTLE DANGEROUS, INDEX AND GLOSSARY. } 2 vols.

TALES OF A GRANDFATHER. *In Press.*

LIFE. By J. G. Lockhart. *In Press.*

Thomas De Quincey.

CONFESSIONS OF AN ENGLISH OPIUM-EATER, AND SUSPIRIA DE PROFUNDIS. With Portrait. 75 cents.

BIOGRAPHICAL ESSAYS. 75 cents.

MISCELLANEOUS ESSAYS. 75 cents.

THE CÆSARS. 75 cents.

LITERARY REMINISCENCES. 2 vols. $1.50.

NARRATIVE AND MISCELLANEOUS PAPERS. 2 vols. $1.50.

ESSAYS ON THE POETS, &c. 1 vol. 16mo. 75 cents.

HISTORICAL AND CRITICAL ESSAYS. 2 vols. $1.50.

AUTOBIOGRAPHIC SKETCHES. 1 vol. 75 cents.

ESSAYS ON PHILOSOPHICAL WRITERS, &c. 2 vols. 16mo. $1.50.

LETTERS TO A YOUNG MAN, AND OTHER PAPERS. 1 vol. 75 cents.

THEOLOGICAL ESSAYS AND OTHER PAPERS. 2 vols $1.50.

THE NOTE BOOK. 1 vol. 75 cents.

MEMORIALS AND OTHER PAPERS. 2 vols. 16mo. $1.50.

THE AVENGER AND OTHER PAPERS. 1 vol. 75 cents.

LOGIC OF POLITICAL ECONOMY, AND OTHER PAPERS. 1 vol. 75 cents.

Thomas Hood.

MEMORIALS. Edited by his Children. 2 vols. $1.75.

Alfred Tennyson.

POETICAL WORKS. With Portrait. 2 vols. Cloth. $2.00.

POCKET EDITION OF POEMS COMPLETE. 75 cents.

THE PRINCESS. Cloth. 50 cents.

IN MEMORIAM. Cloth. 75 cents.

MAUD, AND OTHER POEMS. Cloth. 50 cents.

IDYLLS OF THE KING. A new volume. Cloth. 75 cents.

Charles Dickens.

[ENGLISH EDITION.]

THE COMPLETE WORKS OF CHARLES DICKENS. Fine Library Edition. Published simultaneously in London and Boston. English print, fine cloth binding, 22 vols. 12mo. $27.50.

Henry W. Longfellow.

POETICAL WORKS. In two volumes. 16mo. Boards. $2.00.

POCKET EDITION OF POETICAL WORKS. In two volumes. $1.75.

POCKET EDITION OF PROSE WORKS COMPLETE. In two volumes. $1.75.

THE SONG OF HIAWATHA. $1.00.

EVANGELINE: A Tale of Acadia. 75 cents.

THE GOLDEN LEGEND. A Poem. $1.00.

HYPERION. A Romance. $1.00.

OUTRE-MER. A Pilgrimage. $1.00.

KAVANAGH. A Tale. 75 cents.

THE COURTSHIP OF MILES STANDISH. 1 vol. 16mo. 75 cents.

Illustrated editions of EVANGELINE. POEMS, HYPERION, THE GOLDEN LEGEND, and MILES STANDISH.

Charles Reade.

PEG WOFFINGTON. A Novel. 75 cents.

CHRISTIE JOHNSTONE. A Novel. 75 cents.

CLOUDS AND SUNSHINE. A Novel. 75 cents.

"NEVER TOO LATE TO MEND." 2 vols. $1.50.

WHITE LIES. A Novel. 1 vol. $1.25.

PROPRIA QUÆ MARIBUS and THE BOX TUNNEL. 25 cts.

THE EIGHTH COMMANDMENT. 75 cents.

James Russell Lowell.

Complete Poetical Works. In Blue and Gold. 2 vols. $1.50.
Poetical Works. 2 vols. 16mo. Cloth. $1.50.
Sir Launfal. New Edition. 25 cents.
A Fable for Critics. New Edition. 50 cents.
The Biglow Papers. New Edition. 63 cents.
Fireside Travels. *In Press.*

Nathaniel Hawthorne.

Twice-Told Tales. Two volumes. $1.50.
The Scarlet Letter. 75 cents.
The House of the Seven Gables. $1.00.
The Snow Image, and other Tales. 75 cents.
The Blithedale Romance. 75 cents.
Mosses from an Old Manse. 2 vols. $1.50.
The Marble Faun. 2 vols. $1.50.
True Stories. 75 cents.
A Wonder-Book for Girls and Boys. 75 cents.
Tanglewood Tales. 88 cents.

Edwin P. Whipple.

Essays and Reviews. 2 vols. $2.00.
Lectures on Literature and Life. 63 cents.
Washington and the Revolution. 20 cents.

Charles Kingsley.

Two Years Ago. A New Novel. $1.25.
Amyas Leigh. A Novel. $1.25.
Glaucus; or, the Wonders of the Shore. 50 cts.
Poetical Works. 75 cents.
The Heroes; or, Greek Fairy Tales. 75 cents.
Andromeda and other Poems. 50 cents.
Sir Walter Raleigh and his Time, &c. $1.25.
New Miscellanies. 1 vol. $1.00.

Mrs. Howe.

Passion Flowers. 75 cents.
Words for the Hour. 75 cents.
The World's Own. 50 cents.
A Trip to Cuba. 1 vol. 16mo. 75 cents.

George S. Hillard.

Six Months in Italy. 1 vol. 16mo. $1.50.
Dangers and Duties of the Mercantile Profession. 25 cents.
Selections from the Writings of Walter Savage Landor. 1 vol. 16mo. 75 cents.

Oliver Wendell Holmes.

Poems. With fine Portrait. Cloth. $1.00.
Astræa. Fancy paper. 25 cents.
The Autocrat of the Breakfast Table. With Illustrations by Hoppin. 16mo. $1.00.
The Same. Large Paper Edition. 8vo. Tinted paper. $3.00.
The Professor at the Breakfast Table. 16mo. $1.00.
The Same. Large Paper Edition. 8vo. Tinted paper. $3.00.
Songs in Many Keys. A new volume. *In Press.*
Currents and Counter-Currents, and other Medical Essays. *In Press.*

Ralph Waldo Emerson.

Essays. 1st Series. 1 vol. $1.00.
Essays. 2d Series. 1 vol. $1.00.
Miscellanies. 1 vol. $1.00.
Representative Men. 1 vol. $1.00.
English Traits. 1 vol. $1.00.
Poems. 1 vol. $1.00.
Conduct of Life. 1 vol. $1.00. *Nearly ready.*

Goethe.

WILHELM MEISTER. Translated by *Carlyle*. 2 vols. $2.50.
FAUST. Translated by *Hayward*. 75 cents.
FAUST. Translated by *Charles T. Brooks*. $1.00.
CORRESPONDENCE WITH A CHILD. *Bettina*. 1 vol. 12mo. $1.25.

Henry Giles.

LECTURES, ESSAYS, &c. 2 vols. $1.50.
DISCOURSES ON LIFE. 75 cents.
ILLUSTRATIONS OF GENIUS. Cloth. $1.00.

John G. Whittier.

POCKET EDITION OF POETICAL WORKS. 2 vols. $1.50.
OLD PORTRAITS AND MODERN SKETCHES. 75 cents.
MARGARET SMITH'S JOURNAL. 75 cents.
SONGS OF LABOR, AND OTHER POEMS. Boards. 50 cts.
THE CHAPEL OF THE HERMITS. Cloth. 50 cents.
LITERARY REGREATIONS, &c. Cloth. $1.00.
THE PANORAMA, AND OTHER POEMS. Cloth. 50 cents.
HOME BALLADS AND POEMS. A new volume. 75 cents.

Capt. Mayne Reid.

THE PLANT HUNTERS. With Plates. 75 cents.
THE DESERT HOME: OR, THE ADVENTURES OF A LOST FAMILY IN THE WILDERNESS. With fine Plates. $1.00.
THE BOY HUNTERS. With fine Plates. 75 cents.
THE YOUNG VOYAGEURS: OR, THE BOY HUNTERS IN THE NORTH. With Plates. 75 cents.
THE FOREST EXILES. With fine Plates. 75 cents.
THE BUSH BOYS. With fine Plates. 75 cents.
THE YOUNG YAGERS. With fine Plates. 75 cents.
RAN AWAY TO SEA: AN AUTOBIOGRAPHY FOR BOYS. With fine Plates. 75 cents.
THE BOY TAR: A VOYAGE IN THE DARK. A New Book. With fine Plates. 75 cents.
ODD PEOPLE. With Plates. 75 cents..
The Same. Cheap Edition. With Plates. 50 cents.
THE BOY'S BOOK OF ANIMALS. With Plates. *In Press.*

Rev. F. W. Robertson.

SERMONS. First Series. $1.00.
" Second " $1.00.
" Third " $1.00.
" Fourth " $1.00.
LECTURES AND ADDRESSES ON LITERARY AND SOCIAL TOPICS. $1.00.

Mrs. Jameson.

CHARACTERISTICS OF WOMEN. Blue and Gold. 75 cents.
LOVES OF THE POETS. " " 75 cents.
DIARY OF AN ENNUYÉE. " " 75 cents.
SKETCHES OF ART, &c. " " 75 cents.
STUDIES AND STORIES. " " 75 cents.
ITALIAN PAINTERS. " " 75 cents.
LEGENDS OF THE MADONNA. " " 75 cents.
SISTERS OF CHARITY. 1 vol. 16mo. 75 cents.

Grace Greenwood.

GREENWOOD LEAVES. 1st and 2d Series. $1.25 each.
POETICAL WORKS. With fine Portrait. 75 cents.
HISTORY OF MY PETS. With six fine Engravings. Scarlet cloth. 50 cents.
RECOLLECTIONS OF MY CHILDHOOD. With six fine Engravings. Scarlet cloth. 50 cents.
HAPS AND MISHAPS OF A TOUR IN EUROPE. $1.25.
MERRIE ENGLAND. 75 cents.
A FOREST TRAGEDY, AND OTHER TALES. $1.00.
STORIES AND LEGENDS. 75 cents.
STORIES FROM FAMOUS BALLADS. Illustrated. 50 cents.
BONNIE SCOTLAND. Illustrated. *Nearly Ready.*

Mrs. Mowatt.

AUTOBIOGRAPHY OF AN ACTRESS. $1.25.
PLAYS. ARMAND AND FASHION. 50 cents.
MIMIC LIFE. 1 vol. $1.25.
THE TWIN ROSES. 1 vol. 75 cents.

Samuel Smiles.

Life of George Stephenson, Engineer. $1.00.

Self Help; with Illustrations of Character and Conduct. With Portrait. 1 vol. 75 cents.

Brief Biographies. With Plates. $1.25.

Miss Cummins.

El Fureidis. By the Author of "The Lamplighter," &c. $1.00.

Thomas Hughes.

School Days at Rugby. By *An Old Boy.* 1 vol. 16mo. $1.00.

The Same. Illustrated edition. $1.50.

The Scouring of the White Horse, or the Long Vacation Holiday of a London Clerk. By *The Author of "School Days at Rugby."* 1 vol. 16mo. $1.00.

Tom Brown at Oxford. A Sequel to School Days at Rugby. Parts I. to XI. 12 cents each.

The Same. Part First. 1 handsome volume, 400 pages. Cloth. $1.00.

François Arago.

Biographies of Distinguished Scientific Men. 16mo. 2 vols. $2.00.

Bayard Taylor.

Poems of Home and Travel. Cloth. 75 cents.

Poems of the Orient. Cloth. 75 cents.

A Poet's Journal. *In Press.*

John Neal.

True Womanhood. A Novel. 1 vol. $1.25.

Hans Christian Andersen.

The Sand-Hills of Jutland. 1 vol. 16mo. 75 cents.

R. H. Dana, Jr.

TO CUBA AND BACK, a Vacation Voyage, by the Author of "Two Years before the Mast." 75 cents.

Miscellaneous Works in Poetry and Prose.

[POETRY.]

ALFORD'S (HENRY) POEMS. 1 vol. 16mo. Cloth. $1.00.
ANGEL IN THE HOUSE: THE BETROTHAL. 1 vol. 16mo. Cloth. 75 cents.
" " THE ESPOUSALS. 1 vol. 16mo. Cloth. 75 cents.
ARNOLD'S (MATTHEW) POEMS. 1 vol. 75 cents.
AYTOUN'S BOTHWELL. A Narrative Poem. 1 vol. 75 cents.
BAILEY'S (P. J.) THE MYSTIC. 1 vol. 16mo. Cloth. 50 cents.
" " THE AGE. 1 vol. 16mo. Cloth. 75 cents.
BARRY CORNWALL'S ENGLISH SONGS AND OTHER POEMS. 1 vol. $1.00.
" " DRAMATIC POEMS. 1 vol. $1.00.
BOKER'S PLAYS AND POEMS. 2 vols. 16mo. Cloth. $2.00.
BROOKS' GERMAN LYRICS. 1 vol. $1.00.
" FAUST. A new Translation. 1 vol. $1.00.
BROWNING'S (ROBERT) POEMS. 2 vols. $2.00.
" " MEN AND WOMEN. 1 vol. $1.00.
CARY'S (ALICE) POEMS. 1 vol. $1.00.
CARYS' (PHŒBE) POEMS AND PARODIES. 1 vol. 75 cts.
FRESH HEARTS THAT FAILED. By the Author of "The New Priest." 1 vol. 50 cents.
AYNE'S POEMS. 1 vol. 63 cents.
" AVOLIO AND OTHER POEMS. 1 vol. 16mo. Cloth. 75 cents.
HUNT'S (LEIGH) POEMS. 2 vols. Blue and Gold. $1.50.
" " RIMINI. 1 vol. 50 cents.
HYMNS OF THE AGES. 1 vol. $1.00.
The Same. A fine edition. 8vo. Bevelled boards. $3.00.
HYMNS OF THE AGES. 2d Series. *In Press.*
JOHNSON'S (ROSA V.) POEMS. 1 vol. $1.00.
KEMBLE'S (MRS.) POEMS. 1 vol. $1.00.

LOCKHART'S (J. G.) SPANISH BALLADS. With Portrait. 1 vol. 75 cents.
LUNT'S (GEO.) LYRIC POEMS. 1 vol. 16mo. Cloth. 63 cents.
" " JULIA. 1 vol. 50 cents.
MACKAY'S POEMS. 1 vol. $1.00.
MASSEY'S (GERALD) POEMS. 1 vol. Blue and Gold. 75 cents.
MEMORY AND HOPE. A Collection of Consolatory Pieces. 1 vol. $2.00.
MILNES'S POEMS. 1 vol. 88 cents.
MOTHERWELL'S POEMS. 1 vol. Blue and Gold. 75 cts.
" MINSTRELSY, ANCIENT AND MODERN. 2 vols. $1.50.
MULOCH'S (MISS) POEMS. (By Author of "John Halifax.") 1 vol. 75 cents.
OWEN MEREDITH'S POEMS. 1 vol. Blue and Gold. 75 cents.
PARSONS'S POEMS. 1 vol. $1.00.
" DANTE'S INFERNO. Translated. *In Press.*
PERCIVAL'S POEMS. 2 vols. Blue and Gold. $1.75.
QUINCY'S (J. P.) CHARICLES. A Dramatic Poem. 1 vol. 50 cents.
" " LYTERIA: A Dramatic Poem. 50 cents.
READ'S (T. BUCHANAN) POEMS. New and complete edition. 2 vols. $2.00.
REJECTED ADDRESSES. By Horace and James Smith. New edition. 1 vol. 63 cents.

SARGENT'S (EPES) POEMS. 1 vol. 50 cents.
SAXE'S (J. G.) POEMS. With Portrait. 1 vol. 75 cents.
" " THE MONEY KING AND OTHER POEMS. With new Portrait. 1 vol. 75 cents.
SMITH'S (ALEXANDER) LIFE DRAMA. 1 vol. 50 cents.
" " CITY POEMS. 1 vol. 63 cents.
STODDARD'S (R. H.) POEMS. 1 vol. 63 cents.
" " SONGS OF SUMMER. 1 vol. 75 cts.
SPRAGUE'S (CHARLES) POETICAL AND PROSE WORKS. With Portrait. 1 vol. 88 cents.
THACKERAY'S BALLADS. 1 vol. 75 cents.
THALATTA. A Book for the Seaside. 1 vol. 75 cents.
TUCKERMAN'S POEMS. 1 vol. 75 cents.
WARRENIANA. 1 vol. 63 cents.

[PROSE.]

ALLSTON'S MONALDI. A Tale. 1 vol. 16mo. Cloth. 75 cents.
ARNOLD'S (DR. THOMAS) LIFE AND CORRESPONDENCE. Edited by A. P. Stanley. 2 vols. 12mo. Cloth. $2.00.

ARNOLD'S (W. D.) OAKFIELD. A Novel. 1 vol. 16mo. Cloth. $1.00.

ALMOST A HEROINE. By the Author of "Charles Auchester." 1 vol. 16mo. Cloth. $1.00.

ARABIAN DAYS' ENTERTAINMENT. Translated from the German, by H. P. Curtis. Illustrated. 1 vol. $1.25.

ADDISON'S SIR ROGER DE COVERLEY. From the "Spectator." 1 vol. 16mo. Cloth. 75 cents.

The Same. 1 vol. 16mo. Cloth, gilt edge. $1.25.

ANGEL VOICES; OR, WORDS OF COUNSEL FOR OVERCOMING THE WORLD. 1 vol. 16mo. Cloth, gilt, 38; gilt edge, 50; full gilt, 63 cents.

AMERICAN INSTITUTE OF INSTRUCTION. Lectures delivered before the Institute in 1840-41-42-43-44-45-46-47-48-49-50-51-52-53-54-55-56-57-58-59. 20 vols. 12mo. Sold in separate volumes, each 50 cents.

BACON'S (DELIA) THE SHAKSPERIAN PROBLEM SOLVED. With an Introduction by Nathaniel Hawthorne. 1 vol. 8vo. Cloth. $3.00.

BARTOL'S CHURCH AND CONGREGATION. 1 vol. 16mo. Cloth. $1.00.

BAILEY'S ESSAYS ON OPINIONS AND TRUTH. 1 vol. 16mo. Cloth. $1.00.

BARRY CORNWALL'S ESSAYS AND TALES IN PROSE. 2 vols. $1.50.

BOSTON BOOK. Being Specimens of Metropolitan Literature. Cloth, $1.25; gilt edge, $1.75; full gilt, $2.00.

BUCKINGHAM'S (J. T.) PERSONAL MEMOIRS. With Portrait. 2 vols. 16mo. Cloth. $1.50.

CHANNING'S (E. T.) LECTURES ON RHETORIC AND ORATORY. 1 vol. 16mo. Cloth. 75 cents.

CHANNING'S (DR. WALTER) PHYSICIAN'S VACATION. 1 vol. 12mo. Cloth. $1.50.

COALE'S (DR. W. E.) HINTS ON HEALTH. 1 vol. 16mo. Cloth. 63 cents.

COMBE ON THE CONSTITUTION OF MAN. 30th edition. 12mo. Cloth. 75 cents.

CHAPEL LITURGY. Book of Common Prayer, according to the use of King's Chapel, Boston. 1 vol. 8vo. Sheep, $2.00; sheep, extra, $2.50; sheep, extra, gilt edge, $3.00; morocco, $3.50; do. gilt edge, $4.00; do. extra gilt edge, $4.50.

The Same. Cheaper edition. 1 vol. 12mo. Sheep, $1.50.

CROSLAND'S (MRS.) LYDIA: A WOMAN'S BOOK. 1 vol. 75 cents.

" " ENGLISH TALES AND SKETCHES. 1 vol. $1.00.

CROSLAND'S (MRS.) MEMORABLE WOMEN. Illustrated. 1 vol. $1.00.

DANA'S (R. H.) TO CUBA AND BACK. 1 vol. 16mo. Cloth. 75 cents.

DUFFERIN'S (LORD) YACHT VOYAGE. 1 vol. 16mo. Cloth. $1.00.

EL FUREIDIS. By the author of "The Lamplighter." 1 vol. 16mo. Cloth. $1.00.

ERNEST CARROLL; OR, ARTIST-LIFE IN ITALY. 1 vol. 16mo. Cloth. 88 cents.

FREMONT'S LIFE, EXPLORATIONS, AND PUBLIC SERVICES. By C. W. Upham. With Illustrations. 1 vol. 16mo. Cloth. 75 cents.

GASKELL'S (MRS.) RUTH. A Novel. 8vo. Paper. 38 cts.

GUESSES AT TRUTH. By Two Brothers. 1 vol. 12mo. $1.50.

GREENWOOD'S (F. W. P.) SERMONS OF CONSOLATION. 16mo. Cloth, $1.00; cloth, gilt edge, $1.50; morocco, plain gilt edge, $2.00; morocco, extra gilt edge, $2.50.

" HISTORY OF THE KING'S CHAPEL, BOSTON. 12mo. Cloth. 50 cents.

HODSON'S SOLDIER'S LIFE IN INDIA. 1 vol. 16mo. Cloth. $1.00.

HOWITT'S (WILLIAM) LAND, LABOR, AND GOLD. 2 vols. $2.00.

" " A BOY'S ADVENTURES IN AUSTRALIA. 75 cents.

HOWITT'S (ANNA MARY) AN ART STUDENT IN MUNICH. $1.25.

" " A SCHOOL OF LIFE. A Story. 75 cents.

HUFELAND'S ART OF PROLONGING LIFE. 1 vol. 16mo. Cloth. 75 cents.

JERROLD'S (DOUGLAS) LIFE. By his Son. 1 vol. 16mo. Cloth. $1.00.

" " WIT. By his Son. 1 vol. 16mo. Cloth. 75 cents.

JUDSON'S (MRS. E. C.) ALDERBROOK. By Fanny Forrester. 2 vols. $1.75.

" " THE KATHAYAN SLAVE, AND OTHER PAPERS. 1 vol. 63 cents.

" " MY TWO SISTERS: A SKETCH FROM MEMORY. 50 cents.

KAVANAGH'S (JULIA) SEVEN YEARS. 8vo. Paper. 30 cents.

KINGSLEY'S (HENRY) GEOFFRY HAMLYN. 1 vol. 12mo. Cloth. $1.25.

KRAPF'S TRAVELS AND RESEARCHES IN EASTERN AFRICA. 1 vol. 12mo. Cloth. $1.25.

LESLIE'S (C. R.) AUTOBIOGRAPHICAL RECOLLECTIONS. Edited by Tom Taylor. With Portrait. 1 vol. 12mo. Cloth. $1.25.

LAKE HOUSE. From the German of Fanny Lewald. 1 vol. 16mo. Cloth. 75 cents.

LOWELL'S (REV. DR. CHARLES) PRACTICAL SERMONS. 1 vol. 12mo. Cloth. $1.25.

" " OCCASIONAL SERMONS. With fine Portrait. 1 vol. 12mo. Cloth. $1.25.

LIGHT ON THE DARK RIVER; OR, MEMOIRS OF MRS. HAMLIN. 1 vol. 16mo. Cloth. $1.00.

The Same. 16mo. Cloth, gilt edge. $1.50.

LONGFELLOW (REV. S.) AND JOHNSON (REV. S.) A book of Hymns for Public and Private Devotion. 6th edition. 63 cents.

LABOR AND LOVE. A Tale of English Life. 1 vol. 16mo. Cloth. 50 cents.

LEE'S (MRS. E. B.) MEMOIR OF THE BUCKMINSTERS. $1.25.

" " FLORENCE, THE PARISH ORPHAN. 50 cents.

" " PARTHENIA. 1 vol. 16mo. $1.00.

LUNT'S (GEORGE) THREE ERAS IN THE HISTORY OF NEW ENGLAND. 1 vol. $1.00.

MADEMOISELLE MORI: A Tale of Modern Rome. 1 vol. 12mo. Cloth. $1.25.

M'CLINTOCK'S NARRATIVE OF THE SEARCH FOR SIR JOHN FRANKLIN. Library edition. With Maps and Illustrations. 1 vol. small 8vo. $1.50.

The Same. Popular Edition. 1 vol. 12mo. 75 cents.

MANN'S (HORACE) THOUGHTS FOR A YOUNG MAN. 1 vol. 25 cents.

" " SERMONS. 1 vol. $1.00. *Just Ready.*

MANN'S (MRS. HORACE) PHYSIOLOGICAL COOKERY-BOOK. 1 vol. 16mo. Cloth. 63 cents.

MELVILLE'S HOLMBY HOUSE. A Novel. 8vo. Paper. 50 cents.

MITFORD'S (MISS) OUR VILLAGE. Illustrated. 2 vols. 16mo. $2.50.

" " ATHERTON, AND OTHER STORIES. 1 vol. 16mo. $1.25.

MORLEY'S LIFE OF PALISSY THE POTTER. 2 vols. 16mo. Cloth. $1.50.

MOUNTFORD'S THORPE. 1 vol. 16mo. Cloth. $1.00.

NORTON'S (C. E.) TRAVEL AND STUDY IN ITALY. 1 vol. 16mo. Cloth. 75 cents.

NEW TESTAMENT. A very handsome edition, fine paper and clear type. 12mo. Sheep binding, plain, $1.00; roan, plain, $1.50; calf, plain, $1.75; calf, gilt edge, $2.00; Turkey morocco, plain, $2.50; do. gilt edge, $3.00.

OTIS'S (MRS. H. G.) THE BARCLAYS OF BOSTON. 1 vol. Cloth. $1.25.

PARSONS'S (THEOPHILUS) LIFE. By his Son. 1 vol. 12mo. Cloth. $1.50.

PRESCOTT'S HISTORY OF THE ELECTRIC TELEGRAPH. Illustrated. 1 vol. 12mo. Cloth. $1.75.

POORE'S (BEN PERLEY) LOUIS PHILIPPE. 1 vol. 12mo. Cloth. $1.00.

PHILLIPS'S ELEMENTARY TREATISE ON MINERALOGY. With numerous additions to the Introduction. By Francis Alger. With numerous Engravings. 1 vol. New edition in press.

PRIOR'S LIFE OF EDMUND BURKE. 2 vols. 16mo. Cloth. $2.00.

RAB AND HIS FRIENDS. By John Brown, M. D. Illustrated. 15 cents.

SALA'S JOURNEY DUE NORTH. 1 vol. 16mo. Cloth. $1.00.

SIDNEY'S (SIR PHILIP) LIFE. By Mrs. Davis. 1 vol. Cloth. $1.00.

SHELLEY MEMORIALS. Edited by the Daughter-in-law of the Poet. 1 vol. 16mo. 75 cents.

SWORD AND GOWN. By the Author of "Guy Livingstone." 1 vol. 16mo. Cloth. 75 cents.

SHAKSPEAR'S (CAPTAIN H.) WILD SPORTS OF INDIA. 1 vol. 16mo. Cloth. 75 cents.

SEMI-DETACHED HOUSE. A Novel. 1 vol. 16mo. Cloth. 75 cents.

SMITH'S (WILLIAM) THORNDALE; OR, THE CONFLICT OF OPINIONS. 1 vol. 12mo. Cloth. $1.25.

SUMNER'S (CHARLES) ORATIONS AND SPEECHES. 2 vols. 16mo. Cloth. $2.50.

ST. JOHN'S BAYLE VILLAGE LIFE IN EGYPT. 2 vols. 16mo. Cloth. $1.25.

TYNDALL'S (PROFESSOR) GLACIERS OF THE ALPS. With Illustrations. 1 vol. Cloth. $1.50.

TYLL OWLGLASS'S ADVENTURES. With Illustrations by Crowquill. 1 vol. Cloth, gilt. $2.50.

THE SOLITARY OF JUAN FERNANDEZ. By the Author of "Picciola." 1 vol. 16mo. Cloth. 50 cents.

TAYLOR'S (HENRY) NOTES FROM LIFE. 1 vol. 16mo. Cloth. 50 cents.

TRELAWNY'S RECOLLECTIONS OF SHELLEY AND BYRON. 1 vol. 16mo. Cloth. 75 cents.

THOREAU'S WALDEN: A LIFE IN THE WOODS. 1 vol. 16mo. Cloth. $1.00.

WARREN'S (DR. JOHN C.) LIFE. By Edward Warren, M. D. 2 vols. 8vo. $3.50.

" " THE PRESERVATION OF HEALTH. 1 vol. 38 cents.

WALLIS'S (S. T.) SPAIN AND HER INSTITUTIONS. 1 vol. 16mo. Cloth. $1.00.

WORDSWORTH'S (WILLIAM) BIOGRAPHY. By Dr. Christopher Wordsworth. 2 vols. 16mo. Cloth. $2.50.
WENSLEY: A STORY WITHOUT A MORAL. 1 vol. 16mo. Paper. 50 cents.
The Same. Cloth. 75 cents.
WHEATON'S (ROBERT) MEMOIRS. 1 vol. 16mo. Cloth. $1.00.

In Blue and Gold.

LONGFELLOW'S POETICAL WORKS. 2 vols. $1.75.
" PROSE WORKS. 2 vols. $1.75.
TENNYSON'S POETICAL WORKS. 1 vol. 75 cents.
WHITTIER'S POETICAL WORKS. 2 vols. $1.50.
LEIGH HUNT'S POETICAL WORKS. 2 vols. $1.50.
GERALD MASSEY'S POETICAL WORKS. 1 vol. 75 cents.
MRS. JAMESON'S CHARACTERISTICS OF WOMEN. 75 cts.
" DIARY OF AN ENNUYEE. 1 vol. 75 cts.
" LOVES OF THE POETS. 1 vol. 75 cts.
" SKETCHES OF ART, &c. 1 vol. 75 cts.
" STUDIES AND STORIES. 1 vol. 75 cts.
" ITALIAN PAINTERS. 1 vol. 75 cents.
" LEGENDS OF THE MADONNA. 1 vol. 75 cents.
OWEN MEREDITH'S POEMS. 1 vol. 75 cents.
" LUCILE: A Poem. 1 vol. 75 cents.
BOWRING'S MATINS AND VESPERS. 1 vol. 75 cents.
LOWELL'S (J. RUSSELL) POETICAL WORKS. 2 vols. $1.50.
PERCIVAL'S POETICAL WORKS. 2 vols. $1.75.
MOTHERWELL'S POEMS. 1 vol. 75 cents.
SYDNEY DOBELL'S POEMS. 1 vol. 75 cents.
WILLIAM ALLINGHAM'S POEMS. 1 vol. 75 cents.
HORACE. Translated by Theodore Martin. 1 vol. 75 cts.

Works lately Published.

FAITHFUL FOREVER. By Coventry Patmore, Author of "The Angel in the House." 1 vol. *Just Ready.*

OVER THE CLIFFS: A Novel. By Charlotte Chanter, (a sister of Rev. Charles Kingsley.) 1 vol. $1.00.

THE RECREATIONS OF A COUNTRY PARSON. 1 vol. $1.25.

Works in the Press,

IN ADDITION TO THOSE ANNOUNCED IN THE FOREGOING CATALOGUE.

REMINISCENCES OF SCOTTISH LIFE AND CHARACTER. By Dean Ramsay. From the Seventh Enlarged Edinburgh Edition. With an American Preface. 1 vol. 16mo.

POEMS BY REV. WM. CROSWELL, D. D. Edited, with a Memoir, by Rev. Arthur Cleveland Coxe, D. D. 1 vol.

THE LIFE OF FRANCIS BACON. Founded on Original Letters and Documents. By Hepworth Dixon. 1 vol. 16mo.

THE LIFE AND CAREER OF MAJOR ANDRE. By Winthrop Sargent. 1 vol. 12mo.

POEMS. By Rose Terry. 1 vol. 16mo.

THE AUTOBIOGRAPHY OF THE REV. DR. ALEXANDER CARLYLE. Containing Memorials of the Men and Events of his Times. Edited by John Hill Burton.

SERMONS PREACHED IN HARVARD CHAPEL. By Rev. Dr. Walker, late President of Harvard University.

THE COMPLETE WORKS OF WALTER SAVAGE LANDOR. Library Edition. Revised and Edited by the Author.

BEAUTIES OF DE QUINCEY. Selected from the Writings of the English Opium-Eater. With fine Portrait. 1 vol. 12mo.

FAVORITE AUTHORS: A Companion Book of Prose and Poetry. With 26 fine Steel Portraits.

HESPERIA. By the late Richard Henry Wilde. 1 vol.

HEROES OF EUROPE. A capital Boy's Book. With 16 Illustrations.

BONNIE SCOTLAND. By Grace Greenwood. Illustrated.

THE SEVEN LITTLE SISTERS, who live in the Round Ball that floats in the Air. Illustrated.

www.ingramcontent.com/pod-product-compliance
Lightning Source LLC
LaVergne TN
LVHW012326100826
845148LV00017B/352

* 9 7 8 1 4 2 5 5 2 1 0 5 9 *